Special Praise for *Breaking the Ruhls*

"*Breaking the Ruhls* is a phenomenal unfolding of one survivor's story. Larry Ruhl's deep commitment to honesty in this book illuminates a path for others to follow. A book written for these times of truth-telling."

Peter Buffett
Composer and Philanthropist

"Larry Ruhl shares the details of the inexplicable horrors he faced growing up with astounding bravery, candor, and self-awareness. Predators thrive on silence. By finding the courage to tell this important story, Larry has become a crusader in an effort to bring this pandemic to an end. I'm so glad Larry wrote this book—for the young boy who embodied a shame that never rightly belonged to him, for the strong man who survived carrying it for a good portion of his life, and for countless others who will feel heard and seen after reading these words. Readers will have a new sense of hope, know they're not alone and that recovery is possible. *Breaking the Ruhls* is indeed a gift to the survivors of the world."

Eva Tenuto
Cofounder and Executive director of TMI Project

"*Breaking the Ruhls* is a candid, brutally honest, and refreshingly hopeful story of one man's journey toward healing after childhood sexual abuse. Ruhl never shies away from the truth, vividly documenting the high-highs and low-lows of his everyday life. For many, sexual abuse is a straightjacket that is taken off only when confronted; in doing so, Ruhl proves that life can (and is) to be lived."

Steve LePore
Founder and Executive Director of 1in6

"Larry Ruhl's new memoir is an important act of truth-telling. One in six men has experienced child sex abuse, and Ruhl's sensitive narrative is now a resource for those men as they do the hard work toward healing."

Shonna Milliken Humphrey
Author of *Dirt Roads and Diner Pie: One Couple's Road Trip to Recovery from Childhood Sexual Abuse*

"Larry Ruhl courageously tells the story of the sexual victimization done to him at the hands of his father and emotional and covert abuse by his mother. His memoir offers compassion and hope to all male survivors working on recovery. Larry knows he must share his deepest secrets to recover, and I applaud him for daring to put these truths into the light of day to inspire all of us."

Howard Fradkin, PhD
Author of *Joining Forces: Empowering Male Survivors to Thrive*
Business Partner, Collaborations Training, LLC
Partner Emeritus, Affirmations Psychological Services, Columbus, Ohio

Breaking the Ruhls

Breaking the Ruhls

A Memoir

Larry Ruhl

CENTRAL RECOVERY PRESS
LAS VEGAS

Central Recovery Press (CRP) is committed to publishing exceptional materials addressing addiction treatment, recovery, and behavioral healthcare topics.

For more information, visit www.centralrecoverypress.com.

Publisher: Central Recovery Press
3321 N. Buffalo Drive
Las Vegas, NV 89129

23 22 21 20 19 18   1 2 3 4 5

Library of Congress Cataloging-in-Publication Data
Names: Ruhl, Larry, author.
Title: Breaking the Ruhls : a memoir / Larry Ruhl.
Description: Las Vegas, NV : Central Recovery Press, [2017]
Identifiers: LCCN 2017029851 (print) | LCCN 2017040037 (ebook) | ISBN
    9781942094593 (ebook) | ISBN 9781942094586 (pbk. : alk. paper)
Subjects: LCSH: Ruhl, Larry. | Adult child sexual abuse victims--United
    States--Biography. | Sexual abuse victims--United States--Biography. |
    Sexually abused children--United States.
Classification: LCC RC569.5.A28 (ebook) | LCC RC569.5.A28 R84 2017 (print) |
    DDC 616.85/83690092 [B] --dc23
LC record available at https://lccn.loc.gov/2017029851

Photo of Larry Ruhl by Franco Vogt. Used with permission.

Every attempt has been made to contact copyright holders. If copyright holders have not been properly acknowledged please contact us. Central Recovery Press will be happy to rectify the omission in future printings of this book.

Publisher's Note: This is a memoir—a work based on fact recorded to the best of the author's memory. Our books represent the experiences and opinions of their authors only. Every effort has been made to ensure that events, institutions, and statistics presented in our books as facts are accurate and up-to-date. To protect their privacy, the names of some of the people, places, and institutions in this book may have been changed.

Cover design by The Book Designers. Interior design by Deb Tremper, Six Penny Graphics.

For Jeff Serouya and Linda Kawer
You each took a hand and refused to let me go.

Table of Contents

Preface

As an adult survivor of childhood sexual abuse, I face challenging questions. Is it truly possible to move through the shame I carry every day? Can I have a full life without depending on mind-numbing drugs and alcohol? And the most difficult question of all: Do I tell? But how do I tell? Who do I tell? What happens if I do tell?

My decision to share my story was not easy. It's been suggested to me I'm betraying my father and my family by writing this book. I know now that isn't true.

We live in a society that blames the victim. Shame and guilt are piled on victims, with devastating consequences. Young children are told by the adults who should protect them to remain silent, to keep secrets. Women are accused of "asking for it" if they dress certain ways. Adult male victims keep quiet, guilty for not being "man enough" to fight off an aggressor.

Sexual abuse affects every corner of the population, leading to countless cases of addiction, suicide, eating disorders, depression, and anxiety. And more.

One of the main reasons I'm speaking out is to help erase some assumptions about abusers. My father wasn't the lurking, sinister predator many imagine pedophiles to be. He was a friendly, fun loving, and well-liked guy. That's reality.

By sharing our stories, especially the most painful and shameful pieces, we can shed our own shame and find unity, compassion, and understanding for one another. I've struggled with my sexual identity, addiction, and the wrenching pain of acceptance. Accepting what my father did has seemed, at times, unfathomable. Accepting my mother's betrayal has been equally hard. I was brought up to forgive and forget. I have found ways to achieve the former, but will never allow for the latter.

I am a victim of childhood sexual abuse, but I am also a survivor. The term "victim" speaks to what *was*. "Survivor" focuses on my present and my continued path of healing.

I share my story to help others believe that healing is possible.

PART I: LEVITTOWN

Chapter One

"You're a faggot!" she hissed, spitting out the word, saliva forming at the corners of her cigarette-stained mouth.

Hearing her say that word caused my stomach to churn and my face to burn crimson. She knew she had gotten to me; however, she went on saying it over and over again, mocking me, more enraged each time.

"Faggot. You make me sick, faggot."

Close to tears, I clenched my jaw, grinding my teeth. "Mom, please don't do this."

Silently she moved away from me, searching for another cigarette.

I felt paralyzed. What had changed in the two short days since she told me she loves and accepts me for who I am? I tried replaying in detail what had transpired before this crushing moment.

I had celebrated my twentieth birthday a few weeks before the semester ended at the Fashion Institute of Technology (FIT). As I was packing up my dorm room, getting ready to spend summer break at home, I received a call on the hallway phone from my sister, Eileen. She sounded abrupt and panicked.

"Mom and Dad are going to ask you if you're gay."

"Why?"

She stammered and then mumbled something about always suspecting it but now having proof.

"Proof?" I asked, laughing nervously.

"It's not funny. She went through your room and searched the bags you dropped off last week. She found and read some things."

My heart started pounding.

"Mom said something about a set of envelopes. Does that sound familiar?"

I felt like throwing up. I knew the dangers of keeping private things anywhere near my mother, but in the chaos of the semester ending, I'd forgotten a makeshift journal I had created and left it in a side pocket of my duffel bag. I shuddered at the idea of these deeply personal expressions being read by anyone, let alone my volatile mother. Now, I was being forced to talk about my sexual identity, one of my biggest fears. Eileen and I were incredibly close, allies in a childhood driven by chaos and violence. She was one of the few people I confided in about my conflicted sexuality.

I had an hour before I needed to be on the train. Part of me wanted to run away, but I knew my options were limited. Before Eileen's call, I was resigned to another dreadful summer in Levittown. I had no money and desperately wanted to feel like a normal college kid, who went home to doting parents—a mother who did your laundry and cooked your favorite meal, beaming while you devoured it, and a father who wanted to hear about your classes. I knew this scenario was a fantasy, but I held out hope that it was going to be a decent summer anyway.

All that was over now. How could I turn this situation around? Maybe I would deny the envelopes were mine. I quickly discounted that idea, knowing how many notes, letters, and cards I had written my mom over the years. She knew my handwriting.

Maybe I would say it was a book report for a class, which I knew was only slightly more believable. But as I recalled what I'd revealed in those passages, I knew I was in for a gut-wrenching experience.

Panic rose up through my chest, as dread I recognized from an old place spread over me. It was all too familiar, but I tried to keep it from taking over. I understood the kind of reactions my mother was capable of and wondered if, having previously escaped the worst of her wrath, it was my turn to experience one of her violent fits of rage.

I couldn't stop the memories of what she had done to Eileen from bleeding into my brain. A day from a decade earlier suddenly felt like yesterday.

At fifteen, my sister dated Steven, a slightly older boy who lived down the street. He was Eileen's first real boyfriend, and it was nice having a new face in our intimate family. They often let me tag along with them, which got me out of the house and made me feel like I had a big brother. But over the course of a few months, our mother's interest in Steven grew increasingly obsessive. As a result, she forbade Eileen to see him anymore. It was not the first time our mother's decrees made us miserable, but we knew we had no alternative but to accept them.

It didn't end there. Our mother claimed that hang-up or prank phone calls were coming from Steven. A car driving by slowly, or the sound of a horn honking was Steven sending her a signal.

"He's in love with me," we heard our mother tell our father.

When he tried to convince her otherwise, her temper flared. Our lives morphed into all things Steven. His imagined presence in our house was palpable. Eileen, who was reluctant to give him up, thought our mother wouldn't find out if she stayed in contact with him, writing about it in her diary. One late afternoon, Eileen and I were in the living room watching TV.

Our mother, appearing in front of Eileen, asked, "Did you see Steven at school today?"

Just hearing his name made me tense. After Eileen answered an abrupt no, our mother slapped her across the face with ear-ringing force, knocking my sister to the floor. I sat motionless. Up until that day, she'd only ever hit my father like that.

"Don't you fucking lie to me, Eileen," our mother warned.

As Eileen tried to stand, our mother hit her again, harder this time, knocking my sister into the dining room table.

"Mom, stop!" I pleaded.

"Get out of this house and don't you dare come back until you see your father's car in the driveway. Do you understand me?"

I nodded fearfully and left. At nine years old, I had few friends and was too consumed with worry for my sister to do anything but walk around the block. As I got close to our house, I listened intently to hear anything, but it was hot and the air conditioning, as always, was on full blast, muffling any voices or screams.

After what felt like an eternity, I spotted my father's car barreling down our street. I tucked into a bush nearby and watched him hurriedly get out of the station wagon and disappear through the front door. In that moment, I imagined the entire house bursting into flames, with only Eileen getting out alive, putting an end to this nightmare. I stayed in place for a few minutes longer before heading up the driveway. Was I going back too soon? The thing I knew with certainty was that I couldn't tell anyone. I knew the importance of keeping family secrets.

Nothing could have prepared my young eyes for what I walked into. The house was in shambles: lamps lying on the floor, some of my mother's cherished knick-knacks in pieces, and blood everywhere—on the wall-to-wall carpeting, the coffee table, the sofa. As I turned toward the stairs going up to our bedrooms, my eyes took in the deep mahogany stains that streaked the surfaces, the bloody handprints along the beige walls, and spots where blood had dripped. I sat on the sofa believing Eileen might be dead. My father walked into the kitchen, seeming not to notice me. He turned on the faucet and emerged with handfuls of wet dishtowels. Making eye contact with me, he ordered me to stay downstairs and said, "This is what happens when you lie to your mother."

"Where's Eileen? Can I see her?" I felt numb.

"Upstairs. Wait until I get her cleaned up. If your mother comes back in, just tell her you love her. Okay?"

I nodded and sat and waited. I had to pee but was too terrified to go into the bathroom alone. Eventually, my father came back down, blood-soaked towels in hand, and motioned for me to head up. As I turned into Eileen's room, I saw it too had been ransacked. My sister was on her bed in a fetal position. As she clutched her knees, I saw her face was bloodied and bruised. I wondered where all that blood was from. What had Mother done to her? I stayed in her room and slept on the floor next to her as she cried and groaned in pain.

My family did not discuss the incident. We went along as if it had never happened. Eileen did what she could to conceal the damage to her face, making up excuses when anyone pressed her on what happened.

Weeks later, when Eileen and I were laughing in the back seat of the car, our mother spoke, raising her voice. "Go ahead and laugh at your little jokes, but remember next time either of you betrays me, you'll end up in the hospital. That's a promise." We fell silent.

Recalling that horrible day drove home the enormity of what I was about to face. Stepping off the train, my throat tightened. I could tell that Eileen, who was waiting for me, had already been crying; when I hugged her, she released more tears. Instinctively, I reassured her it would be okay.

My parents were sitting in their regular positions at the dining room table, their expressions both familiar and disquieting. They'd clearly been fighting, and as usual, my father looked defeated. I'd no sooner sat down than my father asked me to join him for a drive and a father-son chat. I managed a half smile and got into the car. I hated the idea of being alone with him, and wondered if this was his idea or hers. Considering he was incapable of standing up to her, I presumed this was my mother's plan. I remained silent as he made his way to a local park.

"I need to ask you some uncomfortable questions."

Uncomfortable for whom? I wondered. *You or me?*

"I hate having to do this, but what's with those envelopes? Do you know what I'm talking about?"

"Why did she go through my stuff?"

"You know how your mother is. She gets ideas in her head. You shouldn't keep that shit around anyway. Who knows who might read it? Are you gay?"

"I think I might be bisexual, but I'm not sure. I'm really sorry, Dad."

I regretted not lying. His look of disgust engulfed me, and I apologized again. He muttered something about being disappointed that I would choose to be that way, and my shame deepened.

"When you talk to your mom, not a word that I told you what she did. Understand? It needs to be our secret."

I did understand. He had been asking me to keep his secrets since childhood.

I braced myself as I walked back into the house. I saw my mother look at my father, and as he nodded, her gaze shifted to me.

"Come out into the garage with me, honey, while I have a cigarette."

I followed her out and after she lit up, she turned and gave me a hug, whispering, "You're my son Larry J., and I will love you no matter what. Now, tell me what you said to your father."

"I told him that I'm bisexual."

"Is that the truth or are you lying to us?"

"No, Mom. That's the truth."

"Do you have AIDS?"

Caught off guard, I abruptly answered, "No."

"Have you had sex with men?"

I nodded yes, but was unsure. Did she consider masturbation sex? Kissing? Getting a blowjob? The lines were blurred, but I was glad I answered yes, based on what I had written on those envelopes.

"What kind of sex have you had with men?"

"Mom, that's personal."

She looked back at me, eyebrows raised in disbelief. "Personal? Nothing is personal as long as you live in my house. Are you doing drugs?"

"No." I answered definitively.

"Show me your arms."

"What?"

"Show me your arms." She sounded exasperated.

"I don't understand."

She grabbed my right arm forcefully and pushed up the sleeve, looking at the underside of my elbow and wrist.

"What are you doing?" I asked, trying not to let my fear and annoyance show.

"Checking for track marks. Drug addicts have them. Don't think I'm an idiot, Larry J."

Shoving my arm aside aggressively, she said, "I don't ever want to talk about this again."

For the next two days, my mother avoided me. Meals were excruciating, as she refused to look at me and disappeared into the garage at times to smoke, leaving me with my father, who also refused any interaction. I was confused and vulnerable, wondering if she had changed her mind about loving me "no matter what." On the third day, she unleashed her fury, telling me what she thought of homosexuality and of me, the word *faggot* puncturing my heart over and over.

After she stormed away from me, I called Eileen, who rescued me by offering to let me stay with her and her husband, Brian, for the duration of the summer. At least I now had a plan of escape; I had always needed a plan. I went upstairs and grabbed my mostly still-packed bags. With the whole summer ahead of me, I longed to be back in the anonymity of New York City, carousing with my roommate in seedy bars and art galleries, two of my new favorite scenes.

I breathed a sigh of relief as I pulled into Eileen's driveway and out of the hellhole of my parents' house. Thankfully, I had a job lined up to keep my mind occupied, and to earn some much-needed money.

I went to work at a home furnishings store in bucolic upper Bucks County. It was the antithesis of Levittown. Winding up River Road, my anxiety settled, and I could focus on handling beautiful objects and greeting customers of a different ilk than my parents and those I grew up with—an escape from what was familiar.

In conversations with clients and coworkers, I avoided giving up any details of where I was from, feeling the stigma of Levittown and the stain it left on me. The first few weeks went along smoothly, with no contact from my parents. In the evenings, Eileen, told me about their fighting, and said my dad thought it was best I wasn't there to hear what my mother was saying.

As the summer trudged along, I developed a friendship with one of the partners of the store. He included me in decisions to remerchandise, and he left me in charge more frequently. After one long weekend, he asked if I might like to join him and some friends for drinks. There was never a discussion about my age, but he knew I had yet to turn twenty-one. While I watched him and his friends order their cocktails with confidence, I felt embarrassed, both by my underage status and lack of knowledge in the alcohol department. I wanted what these people had: self-confidence. Noticing my discomfort, he slid his glass of champagne toward me, and with a wink, he offered me a sip.

My relationship with him developed outside of the business. He started referring to me as his houseboy, which meant housesitting, being his designated driver, and staying at his place after a long night out, along with drunken attempts at sex.

Within a few weeks, I sensed I was wearing out my welcome, so I developed an updated plan. I called FIT and asked what it would cost for me to come back early. I was given a prorated rate, and working backward I calculated how many days I could afford, down to the penny, as my urgency to flee felt dire. I could leave Levittown, hopefully for good.

Eileen felt badly about my decision and wanted me to stay. She felt things could still turn around, as my father had started calling her frequently to check up on me. But I didn't care. I stood by my parents through unspeakable moments, and now they turned against me.

My mom always reassured me our relationship was very special, and even if all else failed, we'd still have each other. She told me I was the only one who knew how to make her feel loved, and for that she would stay devoted to me. Where was that sentiment now? My father's main objective was to please my mother to maintain peace. He needed more love than anyone could possibly give, and he carried himself as a man burdened by rejection.

Right before I made my escape back to the safety of New York City, Eileen called to say my parents wanted to see me. She was afraid if I refused, it would fuel the fire. I was cautious but hopeful that we could have a civil conversation. After a restless night, I drove to meet them at a restaurant. I felt better knowing we would be in a public setting.

Arriving, I immediately felt unsettled. My parents were nestled at a small corner table, with only a handful of other patrons in the restaurant. As I approached, my father stood to give me a firm hug.

He whispered in my ear, "I love you, Son," and I felt my skin prickle.

My mother did not look up, instead staring down trance-like at the menu in front of her.

"Hi, Mom." I greeted her warmly, despite the anxious knot in my stomach.

She said nothing, and my father had a pained look. Quietly, I suggested maybe this was a mistake.

My mother's head shot up. She looked awful, with puffy eyes and streaked mascara.

"A mistake? A *mistake*? You're the fucking mistake," she said, loud enough to make heads turn.

I sat frozen with embarrassment.

"You know what you are? A disgusting faggot." She spat as she spoke. My father tried to quiet her.

"Shut up. Your son fucks men, and you're telling me to be quiet? You both make me sick."

Knocking her chair to the floor, she stormed to the ladies room. I felt all eyes on me, as I slowly made my way to the exit. I was convinced the other diners agreed with my mother. Soon after I left the parking lot, I pulled off to the side of the road, sobbing, letting the shame and humiliation pour out of me.

I made the drive back to Eileen's last as long as I could, weaving through neighborhoods and taking old familiar detours. There I was again, lost in my thoughts, wanting to avoid all human contact. Once home, Eileen greeted me with a hug. There was no need for words.

I kept a low profile those last few days, praying they'd pass as painlessly as possible. The evening before I was to leave, Eileen walked in the door with a worried look on her face.

"They want to see you again."

"You've got to be kidding me."

"No, Dad called and said Mom's a mess. They want us to stop by tomorrow."

My head started to ache, and my mind clouded. Why would I go back there and be humiliated again?

She wants to see you so she can finally beat you senseless, I told myself.

Despite all that happened, I felt an agonizing guilt, which made me feel I had to do what they were asking. I had disappointed them so greatly by not being normal; now it was somehow *my* responsibility to make this better. I felt dirty for having sexual feelings that upset my mother. I knew she felt betrayed. Maybe she had come to her senses and remembered our special bond. I wanted to believe that. I could see my sister felt I had to go. She was, after all, the good daughter who always did whatever they asked of her. I understood it was the easier path, but I secretly wished my sister would stand up to them on my behalf, even just this once.

I tried to give myself another objective to force me back into that house. The only thing I could come up with was that there were some things in my room I wanted to bring back to the city with me. Who knew when I'd ever be back? So I made getting my favorite T-shirt, some music, and a photograph the goal of my visit.

That morning, I was riddled with second thoughts. I imagined my mother hurling more insults, and me hurling my fist in return. I caught myself running with this fantasy, and shook myself out of it with a dismissive laugh.

My father got up off the couch immediately and embraced me when I walked in the house. I stood rigid in his arms, wanting him to let me go. I did not see my mother. I darted up the stairs and grabbed the few things I wanted, overwhelmed with relief that I never had to live in this house again. As I unzipped one of my bags, I caught a glimpse of something in the pocket. I reached in and pulled out a small cardboard folder. It was part of our welcome kit at FIT, and contained a condom and suggestions for safer sex. Listed on the inside of the folder were instructions on needle-sharing habits. This was what my mother had found, in addition to my journal, that caused her to check me for track marks and ask if I had AIDS. I laughed bitterly under my breath and shoved the folder back in the pocket.

At the bottom of the stairs, I turned and saw her on the couch. She was crying, holding her head with one hand and the other in her lap.

"I need to get going," I announced, trying to sound confident.

My mother looked up. I did not see rage, disgust, or hatred. I saw sadness. Incredible emotion hovered over her, and I felt myself softening like I had done on so many other occasions. My father stood to hug me goodbye and slipped twenty dollars into my hand.

"Have a safe trip. Call us when you get settled back in."

He was resorting to his own way of dealing, pretending nothing had happened. He was a master at this.

My mother stood and approached me, stumbling. I wondered if she had been drinking. I knew what was coming next. She expected me to comfort her. I held my arms out, and as she pulled me in close, she sobbed.

"Please don't go."

"I have to, Mom. I need to go back."

"Not today. Please stay a few more days with me. Please, Larry J.?"

"I love you, Mom, but I'm going back." My voice was soft, even as I tried to sound determined.

She cried harder. I looked up at Eileen; she too was crying, but my father looked away. I attempted to break free, but she tightened her grip.

"Don't go. Don't leave me. Please don't leave me."

"I'll come back soon to see you."

"Promise? Please promise me you'll come see me. Just us two for lunch? You'll take me to lunch?" She used her best childlike voice.

"Okay, Mom. I'll take you to lunch." My voice was steady and reassuring. I knew the routine. Despite all she'd said and done, it was now my job to make sure she felt loved.

She followed me outside, still clinging to my arm. Eileen was already in the car, and I was worried I might miss the train. As I turned to pry my mother from me, she broke down into guttural sobs, falling onto the lawn.

"I'm so sorry, Larry J."

I reassured her it was okay, but she kept on.

"I didn't mean to say those things to you. Those words were not meant for you."

Pulling back and looking at her face, I tried to make eye contact, but she couldn't focus back on me. Her eyes darted around into the space behind my head, causing the hair on my neck to stand up. A voice in my head was screaming, *What the fuck is happening here?*

"Mom, what are you trying to say? Please tell me what you mean."

Her hand remained clenched around my wrist, but she refused to look at me. I felt powerless over her as my fear escalated.

"Your father is the disgusting one, not you. I hate him. Do you understand?"

My chest started to tighten, and I couldn't breathe. I needed to get away. I released her grip and turned my back on her. I got in the car. My head swarmed with hazy images of my father and his hovering body. I still couldn't find my breath, and when Eileen asked what our mother had said, I answered her quietly.

"Nothing," I replied. "Nothing important."

As we drove off, my mother remained on the ground, crying.

Chapter Two

In 1962, folksinger and songwriter Malvina Reynolds wrote and performed "Little Boxes," a satirical song about middle-class suburban housing developments popping up across America.

Little boxes on the hillside,
Little boxes made of ticky tacky,
Little boxes on the hillside,
Little boxes all the same.
There's a green one and a pink one
And a blue one and a yellow one,
And they're all made out of ticky tacky
And they all look just the same.[1]

None fit her description more than post-war Levittown, Pennsylvania, a suburb of nearby Philadelphia.

Created by William J. Levitt as an affordable housing option for returning veterans, these assembly line-style homes sprouted up in 1950s New York and Pennsylvania. They came with a long list of conforming requirements—like no laundry hung out on Sundays and restrictions about the types of fences you could erect—in an effort to maintain a cohesive vision. Levitt also refused to sell his homes to black families, his homogenous master plan for neighborhoods extending to the residents who inhabited them. Still, he insisted he wasn't a racist.

---

[1] From the song, "Little Boxes." Words and music by Malvina Reynolds. Copyright 1962 Schroder Music Co. (ASCAP); Renewed 1990. Used by permission. All rights reserved.

But as the houses were resold by their original owners, nothing prevented people from selling to any demographic, and over time the population shifted, with an undercurrent of bigotry still in place.

In our neighborhood, we had one black family, the Robinsons, who had three children. Their son was a little older than me, and the eldest daughter was a peer of Eileen's. The youngest daughter was my age, and we were friends by kindergarten, declaring ourselves blood brother and sister. My parents were the second owners of our home in Levittown. They purchased our house for less than fifteen thousand dollars. Consistent with assembly-line production, it was "made with ticky tacky."

Levitt created six styles for these developments: the Levittowner, Rancher, Country Clubber, Colonial, Pennsylvanian, and ours, the Jubilee. Regardless of the style of home you lived in, you were a "Levittowner" if you lived in Levittown. There was a great divide between Levittowners versus the residents of fancier nearby Yardley and Newtown. That our house was the Jubilee, a name that suggests happy, celebratory occasions, added to the disdain I felt for our life inside those flimsy walls.

The first floor of our house had two bedrooms, one bathroom, a living/dining room combination, and a small kitchen. The modest amount of space let smells travel freely, infusing everything: the coats in the hall closet, the towels, linens, and the rugs often held cooking smells from the kitchen.

On the second floor were two additional bedrooms and a bathroom. The ceilings were sloped in a faux-cape style, making the space feel even smaller. We had an attached one-car garage as well. Other families transformed this space into a family room, but with money very tight or nonexistent, we couldn't afford that luxury. My father made attempts to create a faux family room by hanging cabinets on the walls, placing carpet remnants on the floor, and adding an old table and chairs. However, it was not insulated and was rarely used for that purpose.

The garage was the chief battleground for my parents' fights. It was also where my mother ruminated, while she lit one cigarette after the other. Catching a whiff of smoke informed us trouble was brewing.

One of the better features of our house was the extra-large yard and its proximity around a gentle curve on the street. The backyard was lined with towering pine trees and beds of English ivy, offering me a place to hide and explore. When things got rough inside the house, I climbed trees for hours and watched for signs that things were calm, or, in about half of the cases, worse. Seeing my mother standing in the kitchen was usually a good indicator she was making dinner, and it was safe enough to return. I knew the sap stains on my hands and forearms prompted her to call me "filthy." I hated the way she said that word, and quietly scrubbed myself clean before taking my place at the table.

My mother's taste in interiors contradicted her personality. It was generic and bland, all beige walls and tonal shaggy carpet. The furniture was purchased in matching sets, including a sofa, love seat, and coordinated chair from an outlet center that specialized in cheap furniture in garish floral or plaid fabrics. She collected porcelain figurines and housed them in an illuminated curio cabinet, often playing with them as if they were dolls. The stereo, a piece of furniture unto itself with its console-like configuration and felted, built-in speakers, provided her with endless, often too-loud music. Our tiny kitchen was adorned with copper pots and pans, not to be used, just admired. My parents' bedroom, off limits to us except when my mother tried to get me to take a nap with her, was coordinated with valances covering the windows and a five-piece bedroom suite in dark brown wood veneer.

My mother changed the curtains and switched out accessories, like silk floral arrangements based on the season, taking great care to store them so they were perfectly preserved. She insisted on daily recognition for her efforts. We were to deliver accolades regularly. If we fell short, she made it known through tears, or a meal from of a box, a departure from her frequent efforts at cooking from scratch. It was best for everyone involved to indulge her with praise, warranted or not, as often as possible.

Eileen and I shared the upstairs. She had the largest of the bedrooms. Her room was my safe haven, and I found myself cowering, sleeping, or escaping there on a regular basis. My room was powder blue with a simple twin bed, dresser, and desk. The decor varied. At one point it was a Star Wars theme, which I loved. But in an effort on my mother's part to "toughen me up" and force me to be more of a boy, she tried a set of NFL curtains and bedspread. I hated my bedroom.

Regardless of wall-to-wall carpeting and closed doors, if someone raised their voice slightly, you could hear it as if you were standing next to them. It was unnerving and disruptive. By a young age, I started making forts under my bed or in the deep recesses of my closet as a way to hide from danger. Only then could I sometimes manage to block out my senses.

Eileen and I each had our own set of unfortunate circumstances, based on our bedroom locations. Eileen's was above the living room, with attic space behind her wall over the garage/faux family room. This let the cigarette smoke below permeate her room, and the walls vibrated whenever my mother's fists or hurled objects crashed against them.

My room was directly over my parents' bedroom, the place where many battles originated. The strange sounds that escaped through their ceiling into my room left me covering my ears, and feeling an inexplicable sense of embarrassment. Nothing was sacred, and you had to go to extra lengths to remain unheard—hushed tones, a whisper, using an inside voice. My father understood and learned to master it as necessary; however, my mother simply did not care. She seemed invigorated the louder she became.

———

There are five-and-a-half years separating my sister and me. My mother suffered a miscarriage a few years after Eileen was born, and was unsure if she was willing to try again. My father was desperate to have a son. I had the misfortune of being named after my father, only our middle names and legal first names differentiating us. I was Larry; he was Lawrence.

From the moment I entered the world, Eileen took her role as the older sister seriously and became my second mother, a more nurturing and loving one. When I cried in bed at night, she was the one to come to the rescue. Our sibling bond grew as we found ways to deal with the instability of our chaotic household.

On any given night after supper, we watched TV, brushed our teeth, and put on pajamas. Then I said my goodnights, and Eileen tucked me into bed. Shortly after we turned off the lights, conflict would unfold beneath us. When angry, my mother's tone was scathing and unapologetic. Some nights my father could curtail her rage and get her settled, but on most, there was no stopping her as her anger escalated. When we heard my father urge her, "Be quiet, the kids are asleep!" we knew we were in for a rough one.

My father's words confused me and made me angry. How did he know we were asleep? If he really cared, why did he always let this happen? As their intensity and volume increased, I waited, frozen in place. Would they come upstairs? Had I done something wrong? My mind raced, trying to remember what I did to upset my mother. I sweated with worry and threw the covers off me, only to be left feeling exposed and vulnerable.

As their fighting erupted into an all-out war, I got out of bed and hurried into Eileen's room.

"Are you sleeping?" I whispered from her doorway.

"No. Come in here with me."

Relieved, I ran back to my room for my pillow and a blanket, and found a spot on her floor. I always went to the same spot, under the slanted ceiling next to her closet. It was out of immediate sight as one came into the room, and I tucked up close to the wall, feeling a false sense of protection from it. Eileen and I said very little, listening intently. The argument's repeated theme was our father lying or disappointing our mother in some way, but what we were really listening for was if either of our names got mentioned. We cringed at the thought of having precipitated what was happening between them.

When the energy level became even more charged, I often admitted, "I'm afraid."

"Me too, but you know how they are. It'll be better by tomorrow."

I knew that wasn't true, but Eileen did her best to put me at ease. This night might be behind us; however, "it" wouldn't be better by tomorrow.

Eileen and I had a built in barometer for our parents' arguments. We sensed the moment things were about to turn physically violent, and we jumped up simultaneously, held hands, and raced down the stairs and into the garage.

On our way through the living room, we saw broken dishes and holes punched in the walls. All the lights were on, and even as we shielded our eyes, we saw the mess that surrounded us.

But the worst part was the sound of our mother's blood-curdling screams.

In the garage, we found her pummeling our father's face and chest with her fists. As he tried to gain control and grab her wrists, she went for his face with her nails, knocking his glasses to the floor, pulling his hair, and scratching him, leaving a trail of blood running down his cheeks as it mixed with his tears.

Eileen tried to get between them, which terrified me. I was sure she'd get hit in the crossfire. I screamed, "Stop it! Stop it!" but our mother was so consumed with her thrashing, she either didn't hear us or didn't care. The terror in those moments was unbearable—terror mixed with anger and sadness.

Finally, our father said in desperation, "Karen, you woke the kids."

"Don't you dare say this was my fault when you know the truth. You made me do this."

Our mother was not to be held responsible under any circumstance, ever.

These episodes were often fueled by alcohol. Her drinking added poison to an already toxic imbalance. Her reactions to drinking, always unpredictable, vacillated between extreme childishness and extreme anger. On other occasions, drinking sent her into a deep, tearful melancholy.

She retreated back into the house, slamming the door behind her. She had no use for us.

Our father, breaking down into sobs, asked for mercy.

"I don't know what to do. I love her so much, but she's just so angry. I don't know what I'd do without you kids. You came to your old man's rescue."

He reached out to take us both into his arms, and cried harder.

"Sometimes I just want to die. I don't think she would even care. Would you be sad if I went away forever?"

This led to our pleading for him not to leave us, and we told him how much we loved him and needed him. Together we shared the battle of trying to make Mom happy. He saw us as a special trio steadfast in our dedication to handle our mother, and his wife.

In second grade, I made the mistake of telling my teacher about one of these feuds. I was extremely tired and distracted, and she asked that I stay in the room as the other kids ran out to recess. When she asked if everything was okay, I started to cry. She tenderly gave me a hug, and I confessed that my parents fought a lot and it was difficult to sleep. When she asked if they hit me, I hesitated before saying, "No, not me. But my mom hits my dad." I could see her discomfort, but she insisted it would all be okay. It was not okay.

After dinner that night, our father sat us down in the living room while our mother stayed in the kitchen washing dishes, slamming plates and glasses.

"Whatever happens in our house is our business. Do you understand? If you ever have a problem or need to talk, your mom and I are here for you. We have each other."

I felt hot. "I'm sorry, Daddy. Please don't be mad."

He leaned over, hugged me, and whispered, "It's okay, but never again. Please don't ever do this again."

Was Eileen angry with me too for telling? Once upstairs she spoke to me with fear in her voice.

"Don't ever say anything about her. She could take it out on you next time. Promise me you'll never ever tell again. Promise?"

I did, and as we said goodnight, the conversation between our parents downstairs went from hushed to screaming within minutes, sending the message that no one would tell our mother how to act or what to say in her own home.

On the mornings following a fight, our father was out the door before we left for school, and our mother, still in her robe, face unmade up, sent us off in her normal fashion, with packed brown-bag lunches or lunchboxes, hugs, and the reminder that she would see us after school.

But if it was after a particularly bad night of drinking, the routine was different. Our father went in to work late, and we started the day in a special way. Eileen and I made it a point not to go downstairs to face the aftermath until we were together, hands locked, staring down the stairs as if preparing to jump off a cliff. Our father bid us a cheerful good morning and offered breakfast.

"Your mom had a rough night," he said softly.

Eileen found a way to say we couldn't take it anymore, as he remained on the verge of tears.

"It's not her fault. Your mom didn't have loving parents like you kids have." Despite our pleas for him to try and do something, he defended her.

"Try to be more understanding and patient. She loves you very much. Look at all she does for you!"

He tried to convince us it was him she had the problem with. Eileen was not easily swayed, but she knew not to push. I felt trapped.

Our father was big on "forgive and forget." He urged us to do as he did, and not hold grudges against her. When it came to him, he drove home the same point over and over again: "Love me for who I am. Can you kids do that for me? Please?"

Eileen was Daddy's little girl and threw her arms around him to reassure him.

I knew better than to challenge this bond, so I joined the fold as he broke into a smile and said the words I dreaded.

"Now go in and tell your mother you love her. Bring her some coffee in bed and tell her it's okay."

Without fail, as she nursed her hangover, she cried, waiting for us to say we loved her.

Facing life outside our house was no small task. Eileen and I were adept at making excuses. If a neighbor asked about the screaming, we lied and said we were playing a game late at night. When questioned about our father's scratched face, we said one of us did it by accident playing in the yard, or that it happened at work. If a teacher ever again inquired about home life, we lied. We knew not to let anyone into the truth.

Everything was fine.

Those walls in our house held many secrets. When fists punched holes in them, our father quickly had them patched and painted. We lived in constant chaos, hiding in denial in plain sight, inside our Jubilee.

Chapter Three

My father did not refer to me as "Junior," choosing "LJ" or "Son" instead. In a house dominated by my mother, he saw me as his ally and his buddy, always reminding me of our special, close father-son bond.

"It's best if we follow the 'do as I say, not as I do' rule. This way, there won't be any confusion as to how you should do things. Sound good, Son?"

Nodding in agreement, I won an approving smile from him.

One of my father's biggest fears was that I would turn out to be like my mother, something he liked to remind me of often.

"You're a Ruhl, Son. Don't ever forget that. You'll carry on our family name and make me proud."

One afternoon, my father and I were working in his garden, one of his favorite pastimes. As he dug vigorously into the ground to turn the soil, it was my job to rake it out and smooth the clumps. I wanted to use the rake with the iron tines. Insisting it was too big for me, he relegated me to a small plastic hand trowel. After whining and being told a third time it was too big for me, I slammed my trowel down and declared it wasn't fair.

"That's enough, *Karen*," my father said sarcastically.

I looked up, confused, thinking my mother must have come out from the house.

Seeing my bewilderment, he bent down and leaned toward my face, whispering, "That's right, LJ. From now on, when you act like her, I'll remind you. We can't have two Karens in this house."

His smirk added insult to injury.

I felt myself go red and pushed back tears. "I'm sorry, Daddy."

The idea of being Karen, with her fits of rage and irrational behavior, terrified me. Did he really think I was like her? Besides, she's a girl, and I'm a boy. Could I really be like her? Did he think I was a girl, like people outside our house often thought? I felt ashamed and didn't want these feelings coming back, so I vowed to try my best not to do anything to make him call me Karen, ever again.

I was a skinny, often sickly kid with a lazy eye and big, protruding ears. I inherited the Ruhl ears, my mother liked to remind me with disdain, and I knew from the first time someone called me Dumbo that I had good reason to feel embarrassed.

"Let's see what I can do with these," she said as she placed masking tape across my forehead getting ready to trim my bangs. "We'll just keep it long on the sides." In turn, I ended up with two mounds of shaggy hair coming off of the side of my head in a veiled attempt to conceal my ears.

My longer hair also added to the public confusion about my gender. Being asked time and time again if I was a boy or girl made me want to hide from people. It was a predicament I hated, but even I didn't feel certain about it.

I wondered if I was actually a girl, somehow trapped in a boy's body. I was unsure and kept the question to myself.

My mother knew what she was up against. Should she cut my hair short to make me look more boyish, or keep my hair long to hide my ears but have more people think I was a girl? She made several attempts to solve this, but in exasperation one Saturday afternoon, she said to my father, "Take him to the barber. See if they can do something."

My father did not see any problem. Big ears were, after all, a symbol of his family heritage. As I climbed into the big swivel chair in front of the barber's mirror, he simply told the man with the scissors to give me a crew cut. And so he did.

When I walked in the house and my mother saw me for the first time, she pointed at me and yelled to my father, "What did you do to the poor kid? Look at him!" Hugging me, she started to cry, which in turn made me cry. Once upstairs and alone, I prayed for my hair to grow back as fast as possible. I pulled on it with my fingertips, willing it to grow overnight.

My father was an auto body repairman. He wore a uniform with the company logo and "Larry" embroidered on the shirt. He left for work by 7:30 a.m. and was always home to sit down to supper with his family at 5:00 p.m. sharp.

Playing with cars was about the most masculine thing I was interested in, and he saw this as another way to bond, buying me toy trucks and Matchbox cars by the bagful. While it annoyed my mother, he laughed when I smashed them with a hammer and then, pretending to be like him, faced the task of making them look new. Of course I had no real way of doing this, so he just bought me more, and I continued to bang them up.

My car obsession also kept him from having to give into my mother's pleas to "toughen me up" by throwing a football or baseball, which we both hated.

"He'll end up a sissy if you don't do something," she warned.

But I felt safe and sound in the dirt, with no flying objects. We had enough of those inside the house.

During the summer months when I was off from school, my father sometimes took me to work with him. At the urging of my mother, this gave him an opportunity to mold me into the kind of son he envisioned.

Going to work with him made me anxious. He loved the sad, nostalgic lyrics of country western music and played his favorite station while we rode along, side by side in the front seat. If a song came on about a father and son, he leaned toward me and squeezed my shoulder.

The drive to the dealership was about thirty minutes, allowing for a lot of conversation, confiding, and togetherness. He told me about the problems he had with my mother, and how he just wanted to be loved. He talked about how he had missed out on so much as a kid, with a dad who worked fourteen-hour days and was rarely available.

Once we arrived at the body shop, it was an atmosphere of high testosterone and sexism. Calendars with half-naked women hung above red lacquered toolboxes, and the men sauntered about with a cockiness that was intimidating to me.

"Like Miss June, LJ?" Tom the painter asked, pointing to the calendar.

My face beet red, I nodded and looked around for my dad.

"I do too. She's got great tits."

The other challenge at the shop was the noise. Air hammers gave off a deafening, intolerable sound that shot straight to my nerves. I only covered my ten-year-old ears if no one was looking, not wanting to be a sissy.

The foreman of the shop liked having me around, and while most of the guys didn't like him, he watched out for me, allowing me to hang out in the office when it was stifling hot. I liked pretending to file papers and writing on the three-part carbon estimate worksheets. There was also a female secretary. The guys made jokes behind her back that I didn't understand, but I knew they were dirty. If it were up to me, I'd have spent my entire time hanging out with her, admiring her long legs and piled-high blond hair. But these work days were meant to establish guy time, and my dad couldn't run the risk of me coming home and telling my mother I spent the day with Shelly instead of roughing it with the other men in the summer heat.

I was given old fenders to fix, using the strong-smelling pink compound that was used for dents. I loved playing with that stuff, thinking I was a sculptor creating a piece of artwork. Eating lunch was a different story, as all the guys gathered in a circle, sitting on overturned plastic drums. I dreaded their questions and small talk, knowing in some way I'd be embarrassed. I kept my eye on the clock and counted down the time that was left. Once the day came to a close and my dad clocked out, I sat in the car waiting for the air conditioning to kick in, holding my breath to avoid the lingering scent of chemicals, dust, and my father's sweat. The smell of him nauseated me.

Once home, my mother put dinner on the table for her two men returning from a hard day's work.

"Are you going to go again with your dad tomorrow, honey?"

Put on the spot, I hesitated and shrugged my shoulders. I saw his eyes on me, hoping for my enthusiasm. I did not want to go, ever, but when she insisted she needed a day to herself or he needed some time with his son, I had no choice.

Eileen and I had to be very careful when showing any favoritism to one parent over the other. We naturally fell into the father-daughter and mother-son roles, but the need to bend and adjust based on a situation or set of circumstances was crucial. She and I understood this and did our best to stay out of the fire that was forever smoldering.

For reasons that predated us, the holidays were always one of the trickiest times. It felt like we held our breath starting on Thanksgiving and didn't dare release it until the New Year.

Decorating for the season was no small task, and each year on Black Friday, my mother and I kicked things off by preparing the house. Every surface was cleared. My mother's Lenox dolls and Capodimonte porcelain arrangements were carefully wrapped and stored. The faux candles in the melamine sconces were removed, and the plastic-and-silk-flower-filled baskets were exchanged for more appropriate red and green bouquets. The furniture got an extra layer of polish, and we vacuumed every nook and cranny, changing out the vacuum attachments as necessary and not missing a speck of dust.

My mother was ruthless in these efforts. One of the most daunting jobs I had to tackle twice a year was to clean the felted speakers of the stereo system. She insisted that any accumulation of dust affected the sound, and that was unacceptable during a time when we'd be listening to the Christmas albums of Dolly Parton, John Denver, and Anne Murray. She handed me a box of cotton swabs, and I got to work. I made sure I did a thorough job, as I did not want to disappoint her like my father seemed to do on a regular basis. She rewarded my hard work with a kiss and a hug and reminded me that I was her best boy. I was the only boy, but I knew she was comparing me to my father.

Once she felt the house was ready, she told my father to "get the boxes." He made his way to the garage, set up the ladder, and disappeared into the ceiling through the cutout that allowed access to our attic. That space fascinated me, and as soon as he let me climb up, I spent hours there, hiding and exploring.

The attic was packed with dozens of boxes of Christmas decorations. One by one, we brought them out, reacting with sentimentality as we revealed the contents. This took most of a full week, and Mom remained calm and focused, gearing herself up for those few ever-important days at the end of December. I loved this time with my mother. We were a team, and she was incredibly sweet to me. I cherished it, even though I knew deep down it wouldn't last.

Once her stage was set, and the house was adorned like a winter wonderland in some distorted Norman Rockwell scene, she turned her attention toward the next big task—baking. Each evening after dinner, we would make dozens and dozens of cookies, staying up way past my normal bedtime: decorated icebox cookies, miniature fruitcakes, rice crispy rounds, melt-away wafers with pastel filling, and a crumbly, buttery bar cookie that she would cut into perfect squares.

She needed my help, which made me feel important.

The last piece of the holiday assemblage was to make our lists for Santa. Eileen rarely asked for much, but I made up for her lackluster requests. Regardless of how extensive mine became, our mother's was the showstopper.

She wrote it in childlike language, expressing herself with excitement and referring to herself as a good little girl, making notations next to each item. Once it was complete, she recited it to us after dinner, as she put out a special dessert for the occasion. She created separate lists, so there was no confusion when it came to what she expected from her children versus her husband. We knew her list was set in stone, and you dare not deviate from it. She also demanded extra "surprises," things she mentioned or once admired in a store. We were to remember each and show our thoughtfulness by buying them for her.

Eileen and I were assigned small things like socks, gloves, lotions, costume jewelry, and makeup. Our father's list included sweaters, nightgowns from Frederick's of Hollywood, perfumes, dresses, lingerie, shoes, purses, and on occasion, something for the house, but that would be a specific request. You didn't dare buy her something utilitarian. One year he surprised her with a toaster after she complained the one she had burned everything! By week's end, it was smashed against the wall, as she berated him for the thoughtless gift, telling him to make his own fucking toast. She held an arsenal of grudges. We didn't want to provide her with more ammunition.

As December crept along, approaching those magical days, she slowly unraveled. Our father, determined to give us better Christmases than either of them had as children, ignored any signs of tension building. Little outbursts were treated with an early gift or two. To combat our mother's exhaustion from all the work she did to make his holiday special, he ordered pizza delivered to the door multiple times a week.

The warnings were there. Eileen and I felt the brewing of a dark and dangerous storm, but there was no recourse other than to let it gather and take cover when it hit.

My first Christmas Eves were spent at my uncle and aunt's house on my father's side, along with my cousins. Though a feud generated by our mother later ended this, holidays with extended family were always fun.

They lived in a two-family row home twenty minutes away. While our cousins, whom we didn't get to see often, entertained Eileen and me, the grownups would talk, drink, and smoke. Their massive tree stretched all the way to the ceiling and was covered in mounds of silver tinsel. To complete the atmosphere, the television featured the holiday Yule Log. The highlight of the evening came when all of us gathered in the living room for a family rendition of "The Twelve Days of Christmas." It felt festive, but inevitably my mother struggled to keep up, slurring her words. At her turn to chime in with nine ladies dancing, the refrain she insisted on year after year, she blurted out, "I'm one of them, a lady dancing!"

As everyone laughed, her smile faded and her laughing abruptly ended. She pulled away from my father, pushing his hand off her knee with a not-so-gentle shove to catch his attention. No one understood the spiral we were sliding down except Eileen, our father, and me. By the time he said it was getting late and we needed to head home so Santa could come, she was drunk and looking for a fight. The silence on the ride home was the worst part, knowing her mind was spinning out of control, fueled by rage and alcohol. Maybe, just maybe, she could keep everything inside until we were at least out of the car and safe. I hoped for small victories like that. If our mother flew into a tirade while he was driving, our father often swerved as he accelerated.

As we pulled into the driveway, she was first out of the car, waiting for him to unlock the front door for her. Eileen and I headed up the stairs, but our dad stopped us with, "Don't forget to leave cookies and milk for Santa!"

This was another futile attempt at normalcy. We quickly placed the milk and cookies and hugged our father goodnight. We did not attempt to see our mother. We were in dangerous territory now. Once upstairs, I went straight for Eileen's room with my pillow and blankets.

On Christmas morning, Eileen and I gingerly walked down the stairs together. Despite what had happened the night before, it was still Christmas morning, and I was apprehensively excited. The first sign that it was indeed Christmas were the jam-packed stockings hanging along the staircase. Our father managed to not only eat the cookies and drink the milk we left for Santa, but also to retrieve all the expertly hidden presents, filling the room with colorfully wrapped packages, all shapes and sizes piled high, spread out far and wide.

As we emerged, there he was, moving around, making everything look perfect. This also meant picking up broken glass and anything that had been overturned, remnants of what had been thrown at him. Our mother often took aim at the tree. It represented something hateful to her, and on more than one Christmas Eve, she had managed to throw the tree to the floor. At least now it was still standing, albeit littered with half-burnt cigarettes.

"Merry Christmas!" he announced, not looking at us yet. "Your mom had a bad night, but she's okay now. Why don't we surprise her with breakfast in bed and then we can open presents?"

We knew we didn't have a choice. Christmas could not possibly start until she was sitting amongst the mountain of gifts. This was, after all, all for her.

Handing us a mug of coffee and a piece of toasted stollen, he added, "Tell her you're sorry. She needs to hear that more than anything right now. Please, do it for me."

This command was not up for discussion. Seeing her in her nightgown, with puffy, stained eyes, holding her head, I felt sorry for her. I also wanted to start Christmas.

"Merry Christmas, Mom," Eileen and I offered up. "We brought you breakfast." She forced a smile but remained silent.

"We are really sorry, Mommy."

Releasing pent-up tears, she reached out her arms to hug us and tell us how much she loved us. As she sipped her coffee and nibbled her stollen, her spirits started to lift, and she asked if we were ready to get started.

For hours on end, and one at a time, we opened gifts. Whether or not we were pleased with what was hidden under the wrapping, we showed excitement and appreciation. As Mom unwrapped hers, however, we all watched with caution. She checked sizes, smelled perfumes, felt fabrics, and when she opened something that was meant as a surprise, she dissolved into tears saying how much she loved it. As she opened her sexy lingerie, I was told to cover my eyes and look away. They made jokes about what was inside, suggestions as to what my father had in mind when he chose red or lace, or a negligée that purposefully didn't come with matching panties.

As Christmas came to a close, a calm settled over our house. The day was now behind us, as was the month-long frenetic build up. While my mother was unpredictable at any given moment, something about concluding the holiday released her from some painful memory or anxiety.

My father was defeated and run down from all his attempts at peace and harmony. He sought his comfort, alone with me, upstairs.

Chapter Four

The walk to and from elementary school was a little less than a mile each way. I spent most of those years making that journey with my friend Trisha, laughing and whispering curse words under our breath. Part of the daily trek took us along a busy parkway, with a constant stream of cars rushing by. Silently I worried. What if one of the cars stopped? What if a stranger tried to give us a ride? These fears lessened when she was with me. On the days I had to go it alone, it was unbearable, as I worried about who might be following.

I was constantly troubled by the events at home, and that worry revealed itself in the form of stomachaches and headaches. I envied the other kids who laughed and played in groups, fearless and happy. The flood of uncertainty that filled the house made it impossible to feel at ease. I spent much of the day consumed with what happened the night before, or worse, what was yet to come. While I was eager for class to end and to see my mom, I never knew which mom would be waiting for me.

There were days that my apprehension immediately dissipated when I saw her at the front door, arms outstretched. Sometimes she asked about my day, and I gave her a quick report of the highlights, knowing I wouldn't have her attention for too long. I wanted my mommy for as long as she was willing to listen.

I worshipped her when she could be there, and longed for her when she couldn't.

On other days, the curtains were pulled shut and the front door closed tight as I walked up the driveway. The familiar sound of Johnny Mathis oozed from inside. "When Sonny Gets Blue," "Chances Are,"

or "Twelfth of Never" made my small-framed body tense. She was in
her recliner, slouched down, holding her head with one hand. Her face
gave away the pain and sorrow she felt, her eyes swollen and cheeks
stained with mascara. Her hair, usually teased and lacquered in Aqua
Net, was matted down close to her scalp. A pack of cigarettes and a
filled ashtray were nearby. She had been drinking, but I rarely saw the
evidence. Hearing the door, she looked up and coarsely asked how my
day was. Regardless of how I answered, she wouldn't hear me.

She reached out to pull me in, attempting a loving embrace, the
stench of booze and smoke assaulting me. My mind said *run, get away*,
but I knew to be careful not to hurt her feelings. The house felt like
a cage—sun barely filtering in from behind the draped windows, the
sound of the scratchy records, and a stifling lack of air. I learned to act
quickly in those moments. Bringing her flowers almost always brought
a smile to her face despite how paltry and homegrown the selection
might be.

Those afternoons frightened me, especially when we were alone.
Coming back in to give her the flowers, I saw she was no longer in the
chair. I heard her mumbling angrily from the bedroom, and hoping it
was safe, I quietly approached the door, blossoms in hand. I forced a
smile despite my fear.

Her face contorted in that strange way before she cried—brow
furrowed, lips pulled in, eyes narrowing.

"My special, special boy. I love you so much. You always know just
what to do to make Mommy happy. Come sit with me."

As she reached out her hands, they were trembling. Wrapping her
arms around me seemed to calm her.

Our mother liked to remind Eileen and me how lucky we were to
have the parents we did. Before she started in on one of her stories, she
told us we couldn't imagine what it was like for her as a child.

She loved animals but never was allowed a pet. Reluctantly, her
parents permitted her to have Josephine, a young chicken she discovered
roaming the neighborhood. She doted on her and carried her around,
calling Josephine her best friend, but while my mother was at school,
my grandparents had Josephine slaughtered. At dinner they served

Josephine to my mother, waiting until the flesh was in her mouth before mocking her and asking how it felt to be eating her best friend.

Hearing these stories made me hate and fear my grandparents, and I dreaded their visits. My grandfather was abusive, and I understood my mother's lifelong fear of him. My grandmother Gertrude was controlling and demanded that we all, especially my mother, act a certain way. She combined this with an almost smothering affection, sending a stream of mixed messages and emotions. She gave me a long, firm hug while saying she didn't like my outfit or I needed a haircut. Gertrude berated my mother for not being more ladylike and said she should work toward being a better housewife, that pleasing her husband was the most important thing she could do. Gertrude delivered this missive with a sly wink that made me look away and pretend I wasn't paying attention, but I obsessively paid attention. Gertrude's criticism of my mother's appearance was relentless and led my mother to break into tears. My grandmother never hesitated to call my mother "fat" or to recycle the childhood nickname "string bean," when she was thin.

My mother's teenage years were just as difficult. When she struggled with math or bookkeeping classes, my grandfather hurled things at her, telling her she'd never amount to anything, and calling her a stupid bitch. At sixteen, if she ventured out to a movie or soda shop with her girlfriends, he had her followed by a patrol car. She was picked up from wherever she'd gone and brought to the police station where he worked as an officer. Calling her a whore, he forced her to wash any makeup off her face, as the other officers laughed and called her slut and tramp.

These were the kinds of stories she regaled us with.

Meeting my father changed things. He was kind and patient, and while he came from the wrong side of the tracks, my grandparents approved of him enough to let her date him. As my mother liked to tell me, she saw him coming, latched her claws into him, and didn't let go. In my father's words, he was trapped.

Their wedding took place in a Lutheran Church, one of my mother's first stands against her observant Russian Orthodox parents.

When the odds were in my favor, my mother doted on me. I was sick often, and she did not hesitate to keep me home from school.

Those were special days. I was given a small bell to ring, should I need anything from the layered blanket bed she created for me on the living room sofa. She brought me juice and cheese sandwiches, or ice pops if my throat hurt. I was allowed to watch television all day, and if I felt up to it, she indulged me with a game of Candyland.

It was dangerous territory navigating her moods.

I understood while she claimed to demand honesty, she was actually insisting to be told what she needed to hear. The truth didn't matter, pleasing her did. If she wanted to play a game, you played it. If she wanted to be waited on, you indulged her without hesitation. There was no "I'll do it later" with her. Once, she asked me to take the trash down to the curb. Watching TV, I simply nodded. As I saw her carrying the bags out of the garage, I understood what a grave error I had made. Now meant *now*, and she did not ask more than once. In her usual fashion, she said nothing to me, but the fight that ensued when my father got home, and his coming up to my room to talk to me, ensured I would try my hardest not to make that kind of mistake again.

I learned to become an astute people pleaser. I understood that rewards, sometimes in the form of praise or feeling temporarily safe, came with the expense of trying to make people like me. When I found ways to help teachers or neighbors, I was told how considerate and polite I was. This also took attention away from my ears, and soothed my insecurity about looking like a girl, with my thin, sickly appearance. If I could make people like me, maybe they wouldn't notice how flawed I was.

I did this with kids in school too. If I could win them over by being funny and likeable, maybe they wouldn't call me sissy or leave me out of games. The same skills I used to stay in my mother's good graces applied outside the house.

In second grade, I volunteered to sing a duet with a girl for a concert. At the risk of being made fun of by the other kids, I won the praise of the music teacher. My mom urged me to get involved in sports, but I preferred to sing. Her disappointment had me worried, but I secretly vowed to make her proud. After the concert, the parents gathered around my mother, telling her I sounded "like an angel." Her whole face changed, and she smiled wide, giving me a tearful hug as she told me she was proud of me. My singing brought her the attention of other parents. It was a win-win for us.

When she challenged my masculinity, my father went quiet. Privately, he reassured me I was okay just as I was, as long as I remained loyal to our "father-son bond."

Before I had even started kindergarten, he came to my room after I had gone to bed. It was a painful and terrifying experience as he forced himself into my small body. He said this was part of what made us special, making it clear there was great risk should anyone find out. The undercurrent of fear we all held for my mother made it clear I must obey him.

At school, I tried to navigate bathroom visits, attempting to wait them out, legs crossed at my desk. The fear of another kid or a teacher seeing the dark, bloody stains in my underwear filled me with worry and embarrassment, fueling my determination to hide my secret.

I wondered if Eileen knew, or had the same bond with him. I was too afraid to ask.

For swearing my loyalty to him, he "rewarded" me with kisses that covered my face. On other nights, he made me show him I trusted him, touching my face as he unzipped his pants and entered my mouth.

———

Everyday life as a family meant indulging my mother in a wide variety of activities. She went through a drastic weight loss, dropping from well over two hundred pounds down to ninety. She celebrated her new figure, and loved showing it off even more. When asked how she did it, her standard answer was "sheer willpower." No one dared to mention the diet pills she kept in the kitchen cabinet.

During the summer months, she worshipped the sun. She unrolled her Mylar mat, and reaching for her bottle of Coppertone, she'd ask me to help her, guiding my small hands across her body. I hated hearing her call me outside, knowing all too well what I'd have to do: bring her water or a glass of instant iced tea, and on occasion, pull out the sprinkler and aim it so it rained on her. Once she deemed her skin tone worthy, she wore little strapless sundresses and short shorts with skimpy tube tops.

As part of her new look, her hairdo went from a reddish-brown bouffant to a platinum blonde one. My father was her personal stylist. Pulling on rubber gloves and reading the instructions from the Miss Clairol box, he worked on her, making sure every root was colored as she barked out her demands to be gentler or to dab her face as the dye dripped down. Over time, her private salon nights evolved into full on beauty treatments. She put me in charge of removing the nail polish from her fingers and toes, and scraping callouses from her feet, massaging them with Ice Mint, her favorite invigorating foot cream. She carefully inspected her nails when I declared I was finished. If any trace of the old color remained, she insisted I go over each nail a second time.

Thin and coiffed, she explored her exhibitionist side. On weekends, one of her routine activities was to wash our banana yellow and fake wood grain station wagon. Dressed in a tiny bikini, she filled the bucket with sudsy water and soaped up the car, bending over, spreading her legs, laughing, and making obscene gestures. Knowing how to win her over, I grabbed the Polaroid. She aimed the hose at me while she shifted her hips and chest, laughing, smiling and saying how cute I was.

"Take another one, honey. Look at this!"

The way she played with the hose was unsettling. I couldn't watch her as she put the nozzle between her legs. As she pushed down on the handle releasing the spray, she mocked my father as he disappeared into the garage. Once she finished posing, she looked at the pictures I took. She selected the ones she liked and tucked them away in her bedroom. The others she tossed aside; I then gathered them up and kept them in one of my memento boxes in my room, trying to balance idolizing her and fearing her.

My mother loved to dance. When I was a young boy, she held my hands as I stood on her feet while she did the Bristol Stomp. Once she felt I was ready, we did it side by side, until my feet felt like they were on fire from the friction of my slippery booties against the shag carpeting. She went from giddy to melancholy in a heartbeat, depending on the music she played.

In the early eighties, things changed. She no longer had an interest in the music of her youth because it reminded her of a time she was looking to forget. I was unsure what that meant, but the chill in the air toward my father was noticeable.

One day after school, I saw strange lights on the cement walkway in front of the house. Looking up, I saw a rainbow coming from the living room, and the beat of her stereo system rattled the windows. She was wearing a short dress, and as she gyrated around the living room, the lights from her new plug-in plastic disco ball reflected off the walls. I was filled with wonder and concern.

Sylvester's "Do You Wanna Funk" blared from the speakers. She was in a zone, and barely noticed me as I came in. I felt queasy, but forced a smile to show my approval. She spun around, grabbed my hands and sang out, "If you wanna fuck let me show you how, do you wanna fuck with me." She covered her mouth in feigned shock, and laughed at her provocative word changes.

Donna Summer, The Talking Heads, Devo, Lipps Inc., and Anita Ward were now regulars in our living room as she obsessively vacuumed and dusted mostly during the day when she was alone. Occasionally, the music went well into the evening, leaving me to cover my ears from my bedroom. When the cops came to our door, she flirted, promising them she'd behave. She did not ask me to dance with her as much now that she listened to disco. I was secretly relieved. Her clothes embarrassed me, and the way she provoked my father by flashing her breasts or gyrating her hips made us all uncomfortable. As the heat built up, her sweating caused her blue eye shadow and pink rouge to smudge. At times she looked like a clown. I kept these thoughts hidden, knowing how hurt she would be. In her trance-like haze of loud music and flashing lights, I was invisible to her. Eileen stayed away as much as possible, and my father tolerated it because he had no alternative. We were all relieved when this phase passed.

As the light of the disco ball faded, the light of Jesus took its place. We belonged to St. John's Lutheran Church, always attending the early service on Christmas Eve, before heading to my uncle's, and rarely missing an Easter. We averaged once a month during the rest of the year. In a shift directed by my mother, we now never missed a Sunday. We went as a family. I enrolled in Bible school and went to youth group meetings. I felt safe at church. My mother made casseroles and baked cakes for congregational meetings. My father could not have been happier, his family now involved in something together. He loved anything that gave the illusion of a perfect, loving family.

We embraced the prayers, ceremony, and doctrine of the Lutheran faith. At many services, it was a Ruhl family affair. Our mother, with more confidence than I had ever seen in her, became an assistant minister. Dressed in her robes, she carefully poured the wine from the silver chalice into the shot-sized glasses as congregants took communion. We were a respected family and felt the effects at home. My parents fought less and at one point entered into a weekend intensive group called Marriage Encounter, where they emerged more loving and kind to one another. My mother's wardrobe changed too. Gone were the skimpy outfits with plunging necklines and in came the more conservative print dresses or pantsuits. She toned down her hair color and wore less makeup.

Eileen had friends at church, and joined my father in weekly ushering responsibilities. But she was always more cautious. While she embraced this new life, she knew not to trust it. She had seen more than me, knew better on some level. I got pulled in wholeheartedly. I found my niche in the youth choir and became an acolyte.

The minister's wife asked my mother if she was interested in part-time work helping her while she recovered from surgery. My mother was flattered, and after discussing it with my father, she accepted the job. Normally she didn't feel the need to run anything by him, but she'd never learned to drive, so her job was dependent upon his ability to get her there and back. My mother was excited at the prospect of earning her own money. We would all adjust in order to help her succeed.

In time, she took on a few more church families, cleaning their houses and doing their laundry. My mother, prone to feeling "less than," refused to see herself as a housekeeper, and believed she was doing them a favor, doing good work.

Slowly her attitude shifted, and at the dinner table she talked about the habits of the church's secretary, or the mess the minister's wife left each week. On Sundays, she put her animosity aside to absorb the accolades she received for her performance during the service. By Monday, those feelings had faded.

During a congregational meeting, the minister presented the annual giving report. It reviewed the church's income and called out special donors. A large contribution had come in from one of the parishioners my mother cleaned for, and they were to receive a special commemoration for it. That evening, my mother flew into a tirade about being overlooked by "that bastard pastor." I listened carefully as she chain-smoked and berated the congregation, calling them money hungry. She was furious, and I couldn't believe the hateful words she spewed about the people who were so kind to all of us. Even the choir director was singled out. I worried whether she told these things to anyone else. What would they think of us now?

Soon, what started as an isolated incident for our mother blossomed into a horrible habit. After she was dropped off at her jobs, she went straight for any booze she could find, often blacking out. One by one she gave up or got fired from her jobs. In the midst of the turmoil, she told the minister exactly what she thought of him and his money hungry ways. Our church involvement came to an abrupt end. We were forbidden to return.

If our mother suspected even a hint of talk about reconciliation, we were accused of siding with that hateful man, and she would not tolerate a traitor in her house. We kept our mouths shut. Crosses came off of the walls, and we no longer prayed at dinner. Worried the disco ball would reemerge, I kept it hidden in the back of my closet.

One evening, sounding childish and catching me off guard, she asked if I wanted to play church with her. She had an evil grin that I knew was the result of drinking.

"What do you mean?" I asked, feeling a little nervous.

"We can do the service right here in the living room, like we used to in church. Go on, get your hymnal."

Donning striped bathrobes and creating a procession, she and I reenacted an entire liturgy with my sister and father looking on. She smirked as I recited the Nicene Creed from memory, and we gave communion using grape juice and crackers as the hosts. During the

"Peace be with you" greeting, we all hugged each other. Eileen and my father joined in as we sang "Lamb of God." At the end, my mother laughed. We never played church again.

During volatile times, I longed for ways to connect with her. I went into the hall closet and slipped on her shoes. In the bathroom, I smelled her lipstick, wanting desperately to try it on, but fearing what she would do if she found out. I touched her dresses in her closet and remembered seeing her in each one. I wanted to see my own legs under the sheer white fabric of the dress printed with delicate purple violets. I knew just which pair of shoes looked best with it, and imagined myself standing in the grass, face made up, carefully accessorized, perfectly coiffed. Closing my eyes, I held the fabrics of her clothes close to my face, letting my imagination consume me, offering an escape from what existed just beyond her closet doors.

I discreetly played with Eileen's Barbies. If she played with me, we acted out scenarios including fashion shows, camping trips in the large Barbie Winnebago, and sex. Eileen called it Bex, Barbie sex. Eileen, testing my knowledge, whispered things to me, making me blush.

I wondered if my mother would still love me if I were a girl. I hated when she called me a sissy or told me to toughen up. I wanted her love and approval, and she made it clear I wouldn't get either if I played with girl things. Eileen was more tolerant and willingly played with me, unquestioning, and letting me explore. We hid whatever we were doing if we heard our mother coming up the stairs or calling us from the living room.

Chapter Five

Vacations were an integral part of my father's idea of what a family should do. Like being seen in church together, he loved this illusion of "normal." These adventures took place during our summer break from school, and depending on what we could afford, lasted anywhere from four days to a week. After hauling down our matching red vinyl luggage set from the attic, our mom handed out the suitcases, giving us specific instructions on what to pack, and checking them before we left. On the day we hit the road, I felt relief, knowing at least for the next few days, we'd be away from that house.

Our longer trips took us to Busch Gardens in Virginia, or Sea World in Ohio. After seeing the dolphin show at Sea World, I wanted the biggest stuffed souvenir they had. Eileen, asking for very little or nothing at all, gave me a dirty look, understanding it was a stretch for us financially. I would not be deterred, and after my pouting and whining, my father relented, handing me the fuzzy creature with a wink. Eileen looked at me disapprovingly and whispered, "Don't let Mom see that." We were not permitted to have more than her, under any circumstances.

We stayed in roadside motels, Eileen and I in one bed, and my parents in the other. The first few vacations proved to be great excursions, us singing songs in the back seat, playing games, and looking forward to wherever our next stop was.

As I got older and my mother acted out more, any excursion with her had the potential for embarrassment, as she became more volatile and angry. On the final day of what proved to be one of our last vacations for many years, her wrath turned toward me. In a booth at an International House of Pancakes, after the waitress took our order and

turned her back, my mother started stuffing her purse with the jelly and
sugar packets.

"Don't steal, Mom," I blurted out.

"Don't you dare tell me what to do!"

Storming out, she lit a cigarette. When my father went outside to
try to get her to come back, she got into the car. Eileen, my father, and
I finished our breakfast in silence, and my mother refused to speak to
me for the rest of that vacation. When her back was turned, he'd wink
at me, tousle my hair, and tell me he loved me.

"Learn your lesson, Son?" He'd whisper, making sure she didn't hear.

I hated that he was right.

Our mother was prone to wandering off. At the grocery store, in a
mall, at amusement parks—anywhere we went together, she managed
to disappear. This created a panicked feeling in the three of us over how
angry she might be that *we* lost her. My father did not hide his concern,
and brought me into the dark tunnel of worry with him.

"Stay with me until we find her. I need you."

It was especially frustrating if this happened on a day we were meant
to be having a good time. An outing turned into a Mom scavenger
hunt, as we raced around trying to pinpoint her. Inevitably, she'd be in
tears and frustrated that it took us so long. If my father asked her why
she wandered off, her answer was always the same: "You should've been
watching me."

In 1980, a tremendous buzz happened around the grand opening
of Sesame Place, a Sesame-Street-themed park fifteen minutes from our
house. Kids and teachers alike talked about it in school, and as the
summer approached, my anticipation started to build. The challenge
was I had no one my own age to go with. My mother knew this and
insisted on my dad taking me.

Sporting something boyish, I put on my red Phillies souvenir T-shirt
and a pair of jeans, and we headed out. It was an overcast day, which
added to the morose feeling I had. Making the best of it, I jumped
into the big bowl of plastic balls and ran through the water drenching
playgrounds and mazes. My father laughed from the sidelines and
snapped pictures of me standing on the jumbo waterbed.

When it drizzled, he pulled me into an arcade to play games until the rain passed. Shivering, he stood close with his arms around me as he grabbed the controls. I was pinned between his body and the machine as he pressed himself harder into me. My skinny body felt trapped, and I couldn't breathe; it felt like it lasted forever, and all I could do was hope the PAC-MAN ghosts would quickly eat him.

"Want to play again?" As I shook my head no, he just smiled.

Sitting down to eat lunch, he asked if I was having fun with my old man. As I forced a smile, he grinned back at me, and reminded me to tell my mother all about the great day we had together. I knew I had to, whether it was true or not.

Trips to visit my grandparents were both intriguing and unsettling. Though unlike when they visited us and we felt under attack, going there held other challenges. My mother's parents lived in a house they bought new in the 1940s, and it was kept like a museum. Plastic covered much of the furniture, and the house was meticulous. The basement was as tidy and organized as a hardware store, with coffee-can-lined shelves containing nails, screws, and other necessities. Nothing was wasted, instead recycled with a new purpose in mind.

For larger meals or celebrations the eat-in kitchen couldn't accommodate, there was an extra dinette set in the basement. Stapling fabric to framed-out walls created individual rooms, and the only shower in the house was in a second makeshift bathroom with a curtain as a door. The main floor bathroom was for baths only.

The constant threat of getting an enema by my grandmother terrified me. After a bout of colon cancer, she used them often and extolled the benefits of receiving them. I caught a glimpse of the rubber bag and hose once in the closet in the bathroom, and slammed the door shut, fearful she might force me to endure one. It was the same fear I had for the rectal thermometer and jar of Vaseline, two other things that caused me to panic, because they brought to mind my father's visits to my room. Adding to the already tense environment, their house had the constant smell of cabbage and cleaning supplies.

Grandmom Ruhl's house was the complete opposite: a rambling old place with tobacco-stained walls, worn carpeting, antiques, and a layer of grime covering everything. She lived alone, and the wear and tear was evident. Still, I loved it. I could rummage around for hours, convinced it was haunted and had hidden rooms to be discovered. The basement fascinated me, with its coal cellar and remainders of previous activities, such as curing meats and sausages from when my grandfather was still alive. My father loved that I wanted to be in his childhood home and took me there as often as he could, escaping the tensions of his in-laws. The yard still had its old beagle pens and rabbit hutches, and the grapevines that grew on makeshift trellises were falling apart, but still yielded some tart fruit. The whole place provided endless contrast to the monotony of Levittown.

Across the street, just steps from Grandmom Ruhl's front door, was the neighborhood bar. No trip was complete without a visit there for my father, to check in and reminisce with old buddies, and to show off his son. Picking me up and putting me on the counter, my dad ordered a Scotch. As he nursed it, he offered up the glass to me, as the guys laughed and cheered me on. Tasting it made me shiver, just like when he gave it to me at home when my mother wasn't looking. Here in the bar, just us guys, he let me drink it in plain sight. The men lining the bar were retired steel workers, many of them knowing my grandfather and other now-deceased relatives. The stories were endless, and if I got restless, they let me push the balls around the pool table.

My grandmother had one brother who was still alive, Uncle Rodney. He reeked of alcohol and had a raspy voice. He made me laugh as he tickled us. He slurred his words, causing Eileen and I to whisper, as we tried to figure out what he was trying to say. My mother couldn't stand him, and hid in another room while he yelled out for her, "Where's Princess Karenina? Come on out and see me." By the time he stumbled out, she was annoyed and ready to leave. My dad made excuses for him, but it didn't matter to me. I liked him.

The jockeying back and forth between my grandparents' houses was constant. My mother was free to be herself at Grandmom Ruhl's, but the unkempt surroundings bothered her too much. At Grandmom Ruhl's, we all felt free to do what we pleased. Eileen and I loved to play restaurant, and made elaborate doughs and batters from the ingredients in her cabinets. We created a tremendous mess, but Grandmom just laughed. Our father beamed at how happy we were.

On a few rare occasions, we slept over at his mother's house. My mother refused, insisting it was too dirty, but my father would negotiate a deal so he and I could stay one night during our visit. We would watch television in the pink-walled living room as my grandmother rocked back and forth in her big, upholstered chair, deepening the groove in the carpet from the constant rubbing of her slipper.

As I fell asleep, my father would carry me and put me to bed in the small front bedroom with the twin mattress along the wall. He would crawl in with me to share stories from his own childhood, holding me close as he whispered. He told me about the adventures he had with his friends as a young boy, camping out, hunting, fishing, exploring—all the things he looked forward to doing with me. He told me about his mother's sisters, his aunts, and how much they were loved and how they died. What he told me about his Aunt Emma, dying in bed of a heart attack next to her son, sent shivers down my spine, as he warned that I should always love him because that could happen to him too.

"Wouldn't it be terrible if I left you alone with your mother? I hope you appreciate your old man."

As he pulled me in closer, I would feel him against me, moving, his body tensing then shuddering. I wondered if he was crying.

When money was more of a problem, we'd take day trips to the beach. My mother got to show off her bikini-clad body and enrich her tan, keeping her preoccupied, which meant a reprieve for all of us. My dad had this incredible ability to float on his back. It astonished me how he could remain like that and not sink. He tried to teach me, but I panicked and let my legs sink into the water.

My mom packed a big cooler, and we sat together under the blazing sun, eating peanut butter and jelly sandwiches and potato chips, drinking Fresca. My mother didn't drink when we went to the beach, which let us relax a little more, knowing that the possibility of her lashing out was lessened.

One day my mother told my father to take me to the bathroom to get cleaned up before getting into the car. I had been knee deep in sand looking for crabs and was filthy. Finding all the outdoor showers being used, my dad pushed me toward the door leading into the men's locker room, as panic rose in my chest. The men inside were naked, just out of the showers or changing out of wet bathing suits. I stopped, frozen in place. My dad looked down at me and said something about rinsing off, trying to nudge me toward a shower stall, but I couldn't move. I felt the warm sensation of pee running down my leg. He saw what was happening, and picked me up and took me out, walking me back down toward the water, but far from where my mother was. I couldn't speak or cry. I remained silent as he rinsed me off in the ocean and then carried me back to our beach towels, where my mother and Eileen were waiting.

"Is he okay?" Eileen whispered.

"He'll be fine. Some men were exposed in the bathroom so we left."

Shame washed over me as Eileen looked away. The terror of seeing all those naked men stayed with me. I wondered what that threatening-sounding word meant: exposed.

My father's evening routine, Monday through Friday, never deviated. Home for supper at five, a bath, and then settling into the sofa or a spot on the floor in front of the television. As my father soaked in the bathtub, he often called for me.

"Yeah, Dad?" I asked from the other side of the closed door.

"Come in. But close the door so the steam doesn't get out. Now hand your old man the shampoo."

Climbing up onto the toilet, I slid the heavy mirrored cabinet door open and grabbed the bottle. His gaze remained fixed on me while he touched himself. One hand raised, a finger over his lips indicating that I should be quiet, the other moving quickly in the sudsy water. He just kept talking quietly while I stood there motionless. When he finished, he told me I could go. Sometimes my mother would call for me, and I felt rescued.

When she asked where I was, I answered her the way he taught me. Dad needed more shampoo, shaving cream, or a clean towel.

In fourth and fifth grades, my nightmares came on fast and unrelenting. I had them often, and I woke screaming in terror, lashing out from my bed. Eileen came to my room, and I'd often try to hit her before I was fully awake. Every time it happened, she sat on my bed, holding me tight, telling me it was just a dream as she quietly sobbed.

My father often yelled from the bottom of the stairs, "Jesus Christ. Is he okay? He woke your mother up."

Eileen would put her fingers to her lips, indicating I shouldn't make a sound, as she answered, "He's fine, Dad. Just a bad dream."

After every instance, she helped gather up my pillow and blanket and took me to the safety of her room.

Eileen had her own share of nightmares. My mother liked to tell over and over how Eileen "rescued" me when I was still an infant.

Eileen had a nightmare that someone, or something, was going to hurt me. Taking me from my crib, she carried me to the top of the stairs and shouted, "Catch him! The cats are coming; someone save him!" And as she prepared to throw me down to my parents, my father quietly made it up the stairs, taking me from her arms. He got her settled, and then he alone carried me across the hall, putting his beloved son to bed.

Chapter Six

My mother's attention could either be a treasured gift or a form of punishment. Unfortunately, there was no way to anticipate which it would be. The moments when she was a doting mother left me wanting for more.

As time went on, I had to alter the ways I tried to capture her interest. I picked flowers, washed dishes, folded laundry, and cleaned the house countless times in my efforts to have her notice me. She came to expect these things, diminishing them from special acts of love to now mundane, everyday actions. Her expressions betrayed her feelings. When a smile took over her face, it was usually genuine. When she was about to lose her temper, her faint wrinkles went taut with rage, sending out a visual warning of what was to come.

When a neighbor was sick, I spent hours weeding the cracks in her sidewalk and her front yard flowerbeds. Looking over my shoulder, I could see my mother standing at our front door watching me. I felt sure of myself, thinking how pleased she'd be with me, out doing something kind. I was wrong. In tears, she asked how I could do such a thing, right in front of her. I had helped to beautify someone else's yard while leaving hers uncared for, and that was exactly how she felt: uncared for. Not only had I upset her, I gave her a reason to hold a grudge against me. Sometimes her grudges would last only hours, while others lasted days, but she never let you truly forget. Citing examples years after offenses occurred was a skill she honed.

I was a terrible student. I had difficulty focusing, and the insecurity and anxiety I carried with me manifested itself in my grades. I obsessed over the schedule of quarterly report cards, but if I planned accordingly,

I could make it home and go through the mail before my mother had the chance. I was terrified she would see my bad grades and wanted to avoid the anger she was sure to express.

Worse than the Cs and Ds was the ME (medically excused) notation from physical education (PE). How was I going to explain that I was still getting out of gym months after I had the doctor's note? Getting caught in a lie was not something I wanted to face, especially around such a hot topic as my lack of athletic ability. She made it endlessly clear I was not man enough. My delinquency in gym would give her more ammunition.

Regardless of what the physical activity was, I hated my heart pounding and the increased adrenaline any sport produced. When dreaded swimming lessons started, terror consumed me. The idea of having to change clothes in front of anyone put my stomach in knots. My pre-pubescent body was underdeveloped, and there was the added issue of my ears. Getting my hair wet meant I had no way of covering them up. I pulled at the strands on either side of my head, trying to camouflage them. It was fruitless, and without fail, someone blurted out "big ears" or "why don't you fly away with those things?"

During those hour-long classes, I felt held hostage by the strict, relentless teacher, the penetrating smells of chlorine, and the threat of the changing rooms. Football was almost as bad. I was easily knocked to the ground, and seeing a group of boys charging at me had me collapsing before they even got close. I ran *from* the ball in the air, never toward it. Back in the locker room, I was overwhelmed seeing boys with hair under their arms and on their chests. My body looked pale and weak in comparison.

While out on the field one day, we were instructed to run around the track. I heard snickering as I took off my shirt to change. I kept my gaze straight ahead, averting any eye contact, fearing what might be said to me. As we made our way out the door, the PE teacher blew fiercely on his whistle, and we set off to run. I felt instantly fatigued and struggled to keep up. As I lagged behind, a group of boys slowed their pace and huddled around me. My chest tightened, and I felt my face grow hot. I wanted to cry.

One of the kids pushed me to the ground, knocking the wind out of me. As they stood over me and laughed, I saw the disgust in their faces. I heard the sound of one of them clearing his throat before he launched a mouthful of spit onto my face, followed by the word "faggot." I fought back tears and quickly tried to wipe the saliva from my face and neck as it dampened my T-shirt, leaving a wet spot. Ashamed, I walked back as slowly as possible and lingered long after the bell rang. I changed alone in the locker room and ignored the teacher's glare as I walked by his glass-enclosed office, the thin wire mesh encased in the glass creating a pattern across his balding head.

I spent much of the weekend replaying what happened. I dared not tell my parents. My father wouldn't know what to say, and my mother would either blame him or side with the boys who had done it. My mind raced with varying scenarios, including skipping school, running away, and imagining myself in a terrible accident that would leave me in the hospital. Getting excused from gym class felt like a matter of life and death, and as Sunday approached, my panic worsened. The idea of being in pain frightened me. Feeling exposed and vulnerable, like a waiting target, frightened me even more. I had to take matters into my own hands.

I thought about ingesting one of the paint thinners or fertilizers my dad kept in the shed, but how could I make that look like an accident? I settled instead on inflicting some physical injury and headed out to the garage to have a look around. Nothing was coming to me, and as I grew frustrated, I sat on the floor and stared up at the ceiling. Seeing the outline of the door leading to the attic, I had my answer. Grabbing the ladder, I quietly moved it into place and climbed up. I could feel the sweat forming around my arms and neck as I carefully listened for the sound of the television inside, indicating that my parents were still engrossed in a sitcom. As I got myself into the attic, I turned to let my legs dangle out of the opening. Looking down, I wondered if it was high enough to do substantial physical harm. I closed my eyes and let myself slide out, falling to the ground with not much more than a thud. I stayed there, listening for any sounds inside the house, while scanning my body for pain. Other than my ankle feeling a little sore, nothing of serious consequence had happened. I was onto something, but wasn't there yet.

As my adrenaline started to kick into high gear, I simultaneously felt a calm determination, knowing I had to go through with it. Any pain I experienced was a small price to pay to alleviate the torment that was out of my control at school. Here, in the garage, I was in charge of what I was about to do. I grabbed my father's hammer from the pegboard and went back up the ladder. My hand was shaking as I looked at my feet, my wrists, and my knees—my knee. That was the easiest target. Taking the hammer, I focused on my kneecap and brought it down hard, but not hard enough. It was clear to me that significant swelling and bruising were necessary, to be convincing. With my stomach churning and in a cold sweat, I brought it down again, harder this time, repeating the thrusts faster and trying to block out the incredible pain I felt.

When I stopped to take a deep breath, I rolled up my pant leg to see the results. I was relieved to see purplish-red spots covering my knee as it throbbed. Acting quickly, I grabbed a box from the pile of holiday decorations. My trial jump showed me that I fell too quietly. If I wanted them to believe me, I needed to make noise. With a box of ornaments in my arms, I pushed myself forward, throwing the box out in front of me. As it landed with a crash, I lay on the floor dazed, as my heart raced and throbbed in my chest. I heard my father yell out "Jesus Christ. What in the hell was that?"

After he emerged from the house, he looked down at me in astonishment.

"LJ, what happened?"

Voice quivering, I answered, "I fell."

My mother, standing behind him, started to laugh. Ignoring her, he asked if I was all right.

"I think so, but my leg hurts."

He bent down to have a look. My mother stopped laughing when she noticed the box of broken ornaments spewed across the floor.

"Karen, he's pretty banged up," my father said nervously.

"Yes, but not as bad as my ornaments. Look what you did!"

I felt that old familiar trap of being in a vulnerable position and having her angry. My father quickly added that he would replace them and to not worry. As he helped me into the house, she begrudgingly went to the freezer for some ice. I wanted my mother, but had to settle for my father's compassion. I knew she was angry with me, and this was an inconvenience to her. In that moment I didn't care. She would never understand what I had just done and why I had to do it. No one would.

The next day, I was kept home from school and taken to the doctor after having opted out of a trip to the emergency room. As the doctor examined me, he said it was a bad bruise and I should stay off it for a while.

"You must've landed right on your knee. You're lucky it didn't break."

Nodding in agreement, I became almost gleeful as he suggested crutches and handed my mother a doctor's note, excusing me from gym for three weeks.

When I returned to school, my first stop was to the library, where I made copies of the note before turning it over to the gym teacher. I successfully manipulated that piece of paper time and time again, getting myself medically excused from class for the rest of that school year. While I was afraid of being found out, it was worth the worry, knowing I wouldn't have to endure locker rooms, the confusing smell of body odor, and the endless taunting.

My mother did not have many friends. Her belief was that friends did nothing but hurt you, and she repeated those words to me as sage advice. The closest she got to a regular girlfriend was a woman named Lorraine who lived a few houses away. Lorraine had two sons. The youngest, Robert, was three years older than me. Lorraine and my mother ran hot and cold. When they were in a friend phase, they'd speak in hushed tones over late afternoon coffee. When they were at odds, you couldn't mention Lorraine's name in the house, as my mother seethed with rage over the latest wrong Lorraine had supposedly committed.

Robert showed up at our house often and invited me to play Monopoly or Battleship. I was happy to have a male friend, especially an older one. We attempted a family weekend with them at their beach house, but my mom had too much to drink, and it ended up tense, with my parents heading home early, leaving me behind.

Robert's room had bunk beds, which I thought were cool. As he and I turned in after brushing our teeth and saying our goodnights, he climbed into the upper bunk. We turned off the lights and listened to the chatter of his parents coming from the screened porch. He whispered, asking me if I wanted to play a game. Grabbing a flashlight and a book, he hopped back into the bunk next to me. He directed the light beam below his waist and said, "Touch it." He was so close I couldn't move. Grabbing my hand impatiently, he put it on his pajama bottoms, and when I pulled it away, he told me to keep it there. I was curious and afraid at the same time. He heard someone in the living room, so he switched off the light and we remained silent. As we heard the bathroom door close, he climbed back into his bed, saying nothing.

Back home, Robert was only interested in me coming to his house to play. I'd walk into his room and a board game would be set up on his bed, and we'd each pick a side.

"I got some *Playboys*," he told me in an excited whisper one afternoon.

I'd heard about *Playboy* from kids in school, but didn't really know what it was all about.

"Can I see?" I asked nervously.

"Nah, you're too young. Besides, I can show you what they do."

As he stood up and walked around the bed, he told me to stay on the floor. He looked at his door cautiously as he unzipped his pants.

"Put it in your mouth."

The sight of his private parts and his smell nauseated me. I shook my head no, but he got closer and pushed himself toward me. I started to gag.

"Is anything coming out?" he asked.

I sat unable to move before he thrust himself forward again. I pulled away and thought I might be sick. As he looked down at me, the door opened and I saw Lorraine's face, as Robert turned and quickly tried covering himself. Looking only at me, she told me to go home. I felt the tears start as I made my way down the stairs and out the back door.

When I got home, my mother asked why I was back so soon. I blurted out, "Robert pulled his pants down in front of me." I broke down into tears.

"Go to your room."

My mind raced, wondering if I'd be in trouble. As I heard the front door open, indicating my father was home, my worry intensified. I heard them speak tersely and then there was silence. Nothing was ever said to me about what happened.

———

My father bought me my first gun when I was thirteen years old. It was a BB gun, but the message attached could not be clearer. It was the precursor to me getting my hunting license. I feigned interest in the BB gun and managed to clog it with plastic jewelry beads. I felt terrible for ruining it and dreaded telling my dad, knowing how disappointed he would be. When I made up a story about a neighborhood kid being at fault, he gave me a hug and told me it didn't matter.

He was consumed with the impending six-hour drive to Potter County to indulge in the hunting trips he'd looked forward to ever since I was born. Each time he went on this trip, he came back nostalgic about his high school hunting cronies, as if they were long lost brothers. He'd arrive back in Levittown with venison and rabbit, and while my mother wasn't fond of either, she faked her enthusiasm. It was a rare kindness that she offered him.

The first time I shot a 22-gauge rifle, I thought I lost my hearing in my right ear forever, and I was sure my shoulder was dislocated, if not broken.

"Toughen up, kid," the instructor said to me as he gave me a shove.

I hated guns, and I hated the idea of being trapped in a smelly cabin with strange men, hours away from home.

As the appointed day loomed, my father was beside himself with excitement. We were to be on the road by late afternoon the day after Thanksgiving.

Arriving at the camp, I was relieved to find the bathroom was inside with a door that closed. Taking our things upstairs, I saw my father and I were sharing a room with two beds, which put me at ease, thinking I'd be sleeping alone.

The schedule was predetermined. Saturday was meant for small game hunting, Sunday used to scope out the best place for deer, and Monday was spent in the woods praying for a buck. What I liked best about these trips was sitting down to big home-cooked meals of rabbit and sausages, and playing poker. Blackberry brandy was passed around freely, and my father not only let me drink along, but I even got my own glass. He'd send me off to bed, exhausted from the day. I loved the cocoon feeling of protection my zippered sleeping bag offered.

After my father finished downstairs, I heard his feet on the wood floor as he crossed through the front bedroom into the one we were sharing. After he undressed down to his long underwear, I'd feel the bed sink as he carefully climbed over, nestling himself next to me. Using his foot, he'd try to keep the old springs quiet by bracing it against the wall, steadying the mattress. Once settled, he'd unzip my sleeping bag and pull me close, wrapping his arms tightly around me as he pressed harder into me from behind, trapping me like that until he fell asleep.

In the morning, he was up and out of bed before me, waiting downstairs impatiently as the other guys drank coffee and chatted.

"Hurry up, LJ. We don't want to hold anyone up."

One day, my father yelled "There!" and I quickly raised my gun and shot a rabbit, sending it rolling across the field. There's nothing like your first kill to win the praise and admiration from men in bright orange and camouflage. I got nudged in the shoulder and patted on the back, and once alone, a hug and a kiss from my father, telling me how he'd never been more proud of me.

On the first day of buck season, we were stationed outside before dawn. I was miserable as I shook and shivered in my hunting get-up, the game pocket in my coat heavy with the fossils and rocks I had collected. I prayed that no deer came my way. I heard the crackle of the leaves and saw what I feared most. A young buck standing well within firing distance. As I raised my rifle and got him in my sights, I saw his eyes and his antlers. He was beautiful, standing in an ideal position and offering his wide shoulder. I lowered the gun and made a noise, sending him off down the hill.

My father, seeing all this from a few yards away, walked over and quietly asked, "Why didn't you shoot?"

Shrugging my shoulders, I looked down and said, "I didn't think he was big enough."

He smirked and said, "Okay, Son."

Again in the spring, it was the same guys and the same cabin, except it was trout season. I hated being cold and wet, but surprisingly, I learned to love fishing. The downside was the monotonous long drive, alone with my father, and sharing a bed with him again. I campaigned against going on these trips, but my mother felt it was essential. The guilt she inflicted on me made me feel like a terrible person for suggesting it.

"What if he gets tired driving and gets killed? How would you feel then? Go. Keep your poor father company."

Setting out on a chilly spring morning, we were tipped off to a hidden spot known to have an abundance of trout. Following along a narrow path, we came upon an old trestle bridge. My dad started across, striding effortlessly from one railroad tie to the next, as the terrain below dropped further and further away. As I approached it, I felt my chest tighten. Looking down, the ground blurred, and I became short of breath. I braced myself on all fours, staring down and was drenched in sweat even as frost still covered the trees. Unable to speak, my father unknowingly continued crossing to the other side.

He turned and yelled across the bridge, "Stop fooling around. Let's go."

I remained stuck. I feared that if I made a sound, I would plunge to my death. After yelling at me a second time, he started toward me. I managed to say that I couldn't move, and as he got closer, I closed my eyes and allowed him to help me stand.

"What the hell is wrong with you?"

"Please take me back," was all I could manage. The seeds of my first panic attack had germinated.

═══

My father began to have erection problems. I knew this from my mother's excessive badgering and humiliation.

One of the activities we tried as a family was camping. At first, we all slept in a tent, but as I got older, I whined and complained until we graduated to a pop-up camper with slide-out beds. Eileen rarely joined us in the pop-up, which meant I was alone with our parents.

One evening after I settled in to sleep, the moving camper shook me awake. At first I was startled, thinking something was wrong, until I realized the movement was coming from inside. My mother's demands for my father to "fuck me harder" rang through the canvas walls and into the surrounding woods, where other campers were nearby.

After an abrupt silence, the motion came to a standstill, and she berated him, calling him weak and limp, saying he wasn't a man. She called him pathetic, and as he whimpered, she made fun of him for crying.

One weekend, we all sat around a campfire. It was a rare moment of levity as we laughed and shared stories. As my mother sipped raspberry wine coolers, she passed one to me, reminding me to just take a sip, not more.

"I don't want you to become an alkie," she said, laughing.

I watched her eyes on me, and I felt a pang of fear creep in. She had an expression I recognized, and as she threw rocks into the fire, her pitch became more aggressive. In a heartbeat, her mood disintegrated.

Eileen and I exchanged knowing glances, but my father was oblivious.

"Karen, stop throwing rocks."

Eileen and I remained silent as our mother mumbled. Suddenly, she turned on him, screaming obscenities, calling him a pansy and a fuck up.

Other campers yelled, " Quiet! What's going on over there?"

Eileen and I got into the back seat of the car. Our father wrangled our mother into the front as she tried to push him away. Once inside, he locked her door, and we began a harrowing hour-long drive home, leaving all our belongings behind.

In a dark and sinister voice, she recounted every failure she perceived him having sexually. He gave up trying to quiet her and swerved, almost driving off the road. Terrorized, we told him to be careful. She ignored us completely, as if she couldn't see or hear us. At a stop sign, she attempted to jump out, but my father clutched her sleeve to pull her back in. It was horrifying watching her bloody his face as she thrashed about. I hoped we would get pulled over and the police would save us.

After that episode, my mother seemed to slip away from us more. It was harder to make her laugh or smile. She became convinced that my father's impotence was due to his interest in other women. This made me uncomfortable, as I found it unlikely, but I couldn't contradict my mother, forever needing to stay on her side. She was sure the counted cross-stitch project my father worked on and then gave to the body shop secretary was an act of love. The fighting was monumental as she screamed out, "All secretaries are sluts!"

Her attention then turned to anyone with blonde hair. The Mandrell Sisters, Dolly Parton, and Vanna White all became enemies. If a commercial or program came on TV that included any of them, it was a race to change the channel. If she caught us, we were all conspirators, covering up his lustful feelings. We went to great lengths to prove to her this was not the case. My father smashed his Dolly Parton albums to profess his loyalty, and I commented more often how beautiful my mother looked.

In what seemed like a last resort, my father talked to Eileen about getting help from a doctor for his erections, perhaps to prove it was a physical condition out of his control.

During this all-consuming sexual dialogue between my parents, I was quietly tackling my own. The boys at school spoke of wet dreams and whacking off, but I had not had the former and hadn't experimented with the latter. I pretended to go along with the conversations as though I knew what they were talking about, but in truth, I was clueless. The failed attempt at a father-son chat about the birds and bees still had me believing that babies were born through belly buttons.

I understood the basics. Penis into vagina was intercourse, and that act alone presented a whole host of dangers that we were warned about in sex education classes. Pregnancy, abortions, STDs, AIDS—these words buzzed through my brain like a minefield. Masturbation fascinated me, and the first time I gave in, I worried my own semen could give me AIDS. With so much information to take in, I struggled to make sense of it all. I did know orgasms were both thrilling and unsettling. The more I experimented with them, the more vulnerable I felt. But that didn't stop me. Instead, I lived within tension: the perplexity of desire mixed with desperation to figure out what was acceptable and what was not.

I admired men's bodies, but believed that was unnatural. I focused more on girls at school and tested my arousal around them to be certain I wasn't queer. When I stole my mother's Frederick's of Hollywood catalogues, I found myself focusing on the torsos of the men in the pictures and less on breasts. I hated this, but no matter what I tried, my mind drifted back to men. At the same time, the idea of another man's penis disgusted me. When I closed my eyes to masturbate, I tried to keep images out, focusing instead on the physical sensation, wanting it to end as quickly as possible, only to repeat it over and over again obsessively.

I continued to struggle in school but did what I had to in order to pass. Cheating on tests became a regular occurrence.

I hoped my life was a bad dream, or maybe at any moment I'd wake up from the gas the dentist gave me when I needed those teeth extracted as a young boy. I prayed the past ten years were my imagination.

I fantasized about killing myself. An afterschool special about a boy committing suicide had me mesmerized. It was a way out. The one class I did find tolerable was English. We were given an assignment to keep a journal, and in it, I confessed that I was sad and alluded to having problems. I went so far as to discuss my curiosity about suicide. The teacher's notations assured me there was help to be had with the guidance counselor, but I asked myself, *who is she kidding?* I knew better than to walk into that trap again, and have them intervene with my parents. That was a sure way to make things worse. My friends, mostly girls, told me in notes they passed to "cheer up" and "don't be so sad all the time," but I couldn't shake what I felt.

As I entered my teens, I barely had a whisker, but acne struck, unrelenting.

"What's that on your forehead?" my father asked at dinner one night.

"Larry, don't," my mother tersely warned.

Confused, he just stared.

She went on. "Don't make him feel worse than he already does. It's a pimple."

I was mortified. I'd thought my worsening complexion had gone unnoticed. Of all the things to notice about me, it had to be this?

Thankfully, my voice finished its long journey to a slightly more masculine tone. It was still high-pitched, but I could embrace the vocal quality and label of tenor. I could not resist the urge to sing again, and putting some of my embarrassment aside, found my way into chorus.

When I started singing in my junior year, I finally developed real friendships. While I didn't feel free to be me myself, mainly because I had no idea who that was, chorus was at least a cross section of kids, many of whom had music in common.

In middle school, I scored my first serious girlfriend, and making out between classes became an Olympic sport. This also helped convince the bullies it was real. When she pushed me to go further, I managed a lot of touching, but anything beyond that made me squeamish. Nonetheless, a girl I could label as mine took a lot of pressure off being thought of as gay.

Chapter Seven

The summer leading up to my senior year was a difficult one. I came down with a severe case of chicken pox, which left my acne-prone face even more flawed. It kept me home in the horrible heat, lying miserably on my bed with a fan cooling my irritated body. My mother seemed bothered, as she remained lost in her thoughts of my father's possible infidelity. She spent even more time on her beauty routine, often hours in front of the mirror, mumbling incoherently.

I cared very little about my classes and focused on keeping my grades at passing level. The first week of school, I decided to tempt fate and skipped gym class. As the days went along, I wandered around, sat in study hall, or hung out in the library, tucking myself discreetly between bookcases. As each new week passed, I was both relieved and shocked to have gone unnoticed. I managed this invisible act for my entire senior year.

The kids in the music and theater departments were the ones I related to most. They were creative like me, and with them I felt a sense of discovery in trying to figure out who we were. Here, amongst these kids, I felt less singled out and more accepted for who I was. I could hide behind theatrics and immerse myself in music, which provided me with a great deal of comfort.

This group was made up of all types, which allowed me to be chameleon-like and adjust my mannerisms, way of dress, and opinions based on whom I was talking to or trying to win over. I could pull off looking preppy, and if I got lucky, I could occasionally pass at being trendy. The goth and punk scenes fascinated me, but I couldn't quite get that look right. I attempted to wear flannel shirts inside out and army green pants with safety pins all over them, but I looked ridiculous. I remained vigilant about how I dressed, not wanting to push any limits, but occasionally I got it wrong.

I attempted a black turtleneck with cuffed, pinstriped pants, and shortly after homeroom, was called a faggot. The guy who said it, in a denim jacket and too much scruff on his face, asked me if I knew what that was. I stood there looking down at the floor, desperate to be rescued by a friend or teacher who could diffuse the situation.

"If you don't know what it is, just take a long look in the mirror and you'll see exactly what a faggot is."

Andy traveled in the same artistic circles as me, but I kept him at a distance. His mannerisms were effeminate, and he had a lifetime of being ridiculed as a result. Still, he adamantly denied being gay. He and I overlapped on so many things; it was only natural that we'd become friends. He also had a car, which made me like him even more, and allowed me a way out of the chaos of my house. I got a job at Macy's, where he also worked, and our friendship deepened. He became the closest thing I had ever known to a best friend, but during school hours I played down the friendship, not wanting to be found guilty by association.

Despite mediocre grades and average scores on my SATs, I was accepted to both Temple University and Franklin Pierce College. My friends in the theater department couldn't contain their excitement about their plans to go to such places as Sarah Lawrence, Franklin & Marshall, and Drexel. I envied them as they spoke about the excitement they shared with their parents, reading the acceptance letters over dinner and making plans for the future.

My post-high-school plans were a tornado in my brain, as I struggled with what to do. My mother would not discuss the possibility of me leaving home, and my father looked away every time I asked questions about financial aid or what he might help with. Eileen was moving into an apartment she found with her fiancé, and my parents shared their concern about having the house empty all at once.

I felt desperate to get out, but insecure about being good enough or ready. The sadness that consumed me on a regular basis had me questioning my ability to survive on my own.

With my parents' display of disapproval, I felt they wanted me to fail, and I believed that was exactly what would happen. My mother made it clear she relied on me, and I was the only one who understood her. Privately, my father said the same thing. I was sick to my stomach, as I lay awake at night fantasizing what my life would be like if I left, as opposed to staying home. There was no clear answer.

They agreed to drive me out to Rindge, New Hampshire, to visit Franklin Pierce. My love for antiques and history attracted me to their archaeology department. Even as my father poked fun at me, saying things like, "I knew you'd find a way to stay in the dirt," and "Who cares about finding old shit anyway?" I remained steadfast. The campus was beautiful, and as we walked around, my mother cried and sulked. I felt bad for my father, seeing that he felt out of his league.

The financial aid information from the orientation sat unopened on his dresser. He said the decision to go away was up to me.

"You know how I feel about it, Son," he lamented.

Mustering determination, I confirmed my admission to Franklin Pierce College, but a subsequent diagnosis of the Epstein-Barr virus quickly rendered me too vulnerable, and going away suddenly felt like too much. My father stepped in and offered me a deal: If I stayed home and went to community college, he would not only pay for it, but would also buy me a car. He would tell my mother it was a loan I was responsible for paying back—our shared little secret—as my mother was convinced I was already too spoiled.

I agreed, regretting it almost instantly, I understood I'd accepted a deal to remain enmeshed in their lives, to proctor their fights and remain loyal to each of them, as I had been groomed to over many years. I hated myself for this, and felt I had succumbed to a fate of remaining in Levittown. But I also knew I was staying in what was familiar. I could navigate the intricacies of my life at home.

For the time being, I settled for the devil I knew.

Now married, Eileen and her husband Brian had started their new life. I took over her old bedroom and retained mine for studying. I applied to be a summer intern at a historical society and was accepted as a result of my enrollment in Historic Preservation classes at community college. I kept my job at Macy's, and got my energy back, but my self-esteem hit a new low.

I took long drives in my car, music playing, up and down the Delaware River. I fantasized about living in one of the mansions on River Road, and all the beautiful things I'd fill it with. I thought of a room to myself that was soundproof, with impenetrable walls offering me shelter from all the noise constantly infiltrating my head. I wanted to stop thinking of myself as such a loser, but that was exactly how I felt. I wanted to be good at something, anything, to feel I had a purpose.

The fact that Andy was staying home and attending the same college helped matters a lot, but his curriculum was much more regimented, and I saw him less. I focused on classes that interested me—literature, art history, drawing—but found I had little attention span for any of them. My grades were mediocre, but I didn't care. I spent my Macy's paychecks on clothes, discovering I temporarily improved my feeling of self-worth by wearing expensive things.

I started searching out local antiques auctions. I borrowed my father's station wagon, returning home with furniture, paintings, mirrors, accessories, artwork, and dishes filling the upstairs. I hid things deep in my closets and under my bed, for fear my mother would discover the collection I was amassing. I knew she would feel threatened if I acquired something she coveted, so I did my best to conceal all of it. That came to an end one day when I was at work, and she went upstairs on a mission to see what I had been up to.

When I got home that night, both my parents were waiting for me. My father angrily told me I was not to bring anything else into the house. He was worried the floor would fall through from the sheer weight of what was upstairs. He ended the conversation with a question that made my face turn crimson: "How are you affording all this, anyway?"

I was not about to admit I had discovered the pleasures of credit cards. I justified having them by telling myself I wasn't away at an expensive school, I had a job, and at least I wasn't using drugs. The antiques I bought at auction would certainly only go up in value, and my extensive wardrobe was essential for work and for looking the part of a successful student and antiques collector. It was the only way I felt I had an identity.

A woman in my Asian Literature class caught my eye. She stood out from the rest and was always beautifully dressed. We exchanged nods and raised eyebrows as we read aloud from the *Divan of Hafiz* and *The Rubaiyat*. Mustering up some courage, I asked if she'd have lunch with me, and on a cool, autumn day we laughed and talked about our Levittown upbringings.

Penny made me feel secure as she embraced my eccentricities. We had a brief attempt at romance, but the chemistry wasn't there beyond some sultry make-out sessions. Neither of us was discouraged. We became trusted friends. We relied on each other for creative opinions and support in endeavors that went beyond the scope of what we learned at home. Penny was determined to have a big life in New York City, and I envied her as she shared her dreams to attend the Fashion Institute of Technology and pursue a career in fashion.

With the edict placed on any further collecting, I used the weekends my parents spent away in their camper to enjoy my inventory. Andy and Penny loved coming over to hear the stories of my purchases and why I chose them. I'd play Gregorian chants, light candles, and make tea, serving them out of the antique cups and saucers I kept hidden in shoeboxes. I felt connected to these objects, and they helped me to feel special and not ordinary like the house they were stored in.

Penny asked me to go with her to her interview at FIT. She was nervous, so we spent the train ride talking nonstop about fashion and how her life would change if she got accepted. As we approached Twenty-Seventh Street, the campus came into view and enthralled me. The buildings that housed classrooms looked inviting, not daunting as I had imagined. I gave her a hug and wished her luck as I took a seat on a bench. She and I loved people watching, and it was my idea to take notes on the characters I saw walking by while she was inside. Levittown was so homogeneous and still so white. But here, people from every walk of life strolled past me, and I wondered who they were and what had brought them there.

I stood to stretch my legs and walked toward the main building where Penny had gone. The woman at the front desk offered me a brochure, which annoyed me, as it suggested I looked like I was just visiting. I wanted to look like a New Yorker, not a Levittowner. I browsed through the information and read the list of majors. My eyes stopped at Display and Exhibit Design, Associates of the Arts. I never imagined such a thing existed.

I was creative, not artistic. I loved helping the visual merchandising team at Macy's at Christmas and would've worked those grueling hours for free if they had asked me to. I stared again at the words in front of me. Could I possibly get in? This was the first thing that excited me since attending my first auction. Now, standing here in New York City, perhaps I'd found a solution.

My parents did not take the news well. My mother hated that her son had chosen a design school, a place for girls and fairies, and assured me I'd regret my decision. My father questioned how I could do this to him after all he had done for me, and I could feel my anger rise. I wondered exactly what he felt he had done for me. Feeling my face flush, I did not want him to know he was getting to me, because I knew at any moment he'd call me Karen.

As I tried to calmly explain to him I needed to see what else was out there for me, he asked tearfully why he himself wasn't enough to keep me at home. Conflicted, I shifted from anger to guilt. I had allowed myself to feel excited about my decision, but here I was, letting him down again. As if he felt my weakening, he reminded me I could get a job in Levittown, and it didn't matter to him what I did as long as I stayed with him. He went on to tell me how much he loved me and that he knew this day would come, his own "Cat's in the Cradle." I was reminded of those car rides as a kid, when he woefully sang those lyrics to me, hand squeezing my knee. "When you coming home, son? I don't know when . . . "

I fumbled with my words, attempting to reassure him it wouldn't be like that; I'd make time for him. I didn't believe it myself, but convincing him was my only way out. I told myself over and over to stay strong, that I had to do this. He hugged me before walking away, and I struggled to comprehend everything I was feeling and thinking.

After a few days, he told me that he would do what he could to help. After I thanked him, he couldn't help himself and added that he would hold out hope that I would hate it and return home. I made a promise to myself that I wouldn't let that happen under any circumstances.

———

During the summer before I was to move to New York City, I asked a woman I worked with at Macy's to attend a formal fundraiser at the historical society. Claudia was significantly older, but we seemed to have a strong connection when we saw each other in the break room, laughing at the management or company policies. Although I blushed and stammered when I talked, she agreed with a huge smile. She was by far the most attractive person I had ever met, and my heart raced every time I saw or spoke with her. Her hair was long and almost black. She had large, beautiful dark eyes and a curvy, fit, sensual body.

When she showed up on the night of the fundraiser in her sports car, I was entranced. Dressed in a beautiful black fitted cocktail dress, hair done perfectly, she smiled radiantly. My parents were home which embarrassed me, but she seized the opportunity and greeted them both warmly. My father looked dumbfounded, and I saw my mother's eyebrows rise. I started to apologize for the house, my parents, and Levittown, but she looked me in the eyes and told me none of it mattered. I couldn't contain my smile as we drove off.

We didn't leave each other's side that evening. We danced, laughed, whispered, and avoided the long stares that we got as we flirted and embraced. She looked every bit of her thirty-something years, and I looked young for twenty. I knew my parents had left to spend the weekend at the camper, and as we approached the house late in the evening, my nerves kicked in and I invited her inside.

I paid attention to things Claudia shared with me, like her favorite food, music, art—all things to understand her better. As I played one of her favorite bands on the stereo, she kissed me gently on the cheek. Unable to resist my twenty-year-old urges any longer, I took her in my arms and kissed her deeply. She gasped and told me that she'd been looking forward to that all night. I wondered if I was doing the right thing, and if I'd know what to do once we got to my bedroom. We fumbled and laughed as we struggled to pull ourselves up the carpeted stairs. I stopped for a breath and blurted out that I didn't have a condom, but she quieted me and told me not to worry about such things. We were quick to get our clothes off. Her breasts were even more enticing than I had imagined, and as I took them in my mouth, loving the taste of her, her reaction urged me on. I saw and heard her desire and allowed my excitement to consume me.

Caught up in the moment, I moved on top of her and awkwardly found my way inside of her. She thankfully mistook my clumsiness for teasing. Gaining confidence, I responded to her body's movements and allowed myself to feel incredible pleasure. When she climaxed, I could not contain myself and started to laugh. It was exhilarating, and for the first time, I felt completely normal. This was what sex was supposed to be like. Between a man and woman. The pieces not only fit, but they made sense and felt great when they were put together. I wondered if she could tell it was my first time having intercourse. We remained like that for a few hours, repeating what we had just done until we were worn out. I stared up at the slanted ceiling of what once was Eileen's room, the same room I slept in time and time again to escape what was happening below. Now, here I was, with a woman, an experience I could hardly believe.

Claudia and I continued to see each other as often as we could. She expressed her sadness and disappointment that I'd be going away to college, but appreciated the urgency I felt in leaving. She whisked me away for weekends to charming bed and breakfasts. It was a far cry from the campgrounds and sleeping arrangements I was used to with my parents. My father urged us to visit them at the campground, but I couldn't stand the idea, especially knowing that my mother did not approve of Claudia. We listened to music and fantasized about the type of house we'd live in together. We both wanted a stone house with gardens and quiet corners to read to each other like we had at one of our favorite inns. Money was never a question. Claudia paid for everything, and even when I tried to contribute, she refused. My awe for her and the incredible sense of mystery deepened. Her job at Macy's did not match the person I experienced, but she said the same about my upbringing and me. I was naively in love.

I was still best friends with Andy. Rumors about Andy's sexuality continued to follow him, only now they circled around work rather than school hallways. I wanted to get the truth from him. I had the house to myself one weekend and asked him to come over to talk. I pulled out the bottle of cheap wine they gave me at the fundraising dinner, knowing we'd both need something to calm our nerves.

I hated feeling he was keeping something from me. I took great pride in the personal details I got my friends to reveal, but here was Andy, my best friend, and he was clearly holding on to secrets. While I revealed little, I demanded complete honesty from others. It was a double standard I employed to protect myself. If I knew your secrets, you'd remain loyal to me. If you knew mine, I was sure you'd abandon me.

I cautiously broached the subject of what I heard about him. I reached out my hand and touched his leg in an attempt to calm him, and reassured him that he could trust me. Buzzing from the wine that was almost gone, he didn't pull away and shifted his leg, increasing the pressure from my hand. Seeing that he was aroused started my heart racing. I slid my hand further up his leg and under his shorts. Pushing my hand down harder, he pulled my neck in and kissed me deeply as he struggled to find a rhythm with his mouth. I was caught off guard by his aggression, but didn't want to stop either.

We went upstairs to the same bed I had lost my virginity in with Claudia. I did not pause to consider what I was doing. As he continued to kiss me, his mouth all over my face and neck, he moaned in my ear. Arousal ceased in that moment, as dread and fear took over as I suddenly thought of my father. Pushing Andy away, I disappeared into the bathroom, slamming the door behind me. Andy kept apologizing, asking me to come out and talk. I told him to leave, screamed for him to get out.

I remained on the bathroom floor, holding my spinning head and asking myself what the fuck was wrong with me. Why, on that bed with Andy, did my father enter my thoughts? The disgust and terror that filled my mind and stomach became too much, and I threw up. I could not move, and curled up on the bathroom floor, I quietly wept, confused and afraid.

The next morning, I saw that Andy left traces of his affection all over my neck. I was mortified and couldn't figure out how I would explain it. When he called later that morning, I was belligerent. I put an end to the friendship with words that echoed in my head and filled me with shame.

"You attacked me last night. Don't ever come near me again. I hate you for what you did."

I called Claudia and told her I needed to see her. Hearing my voice, she knew something was wrong. As she sat down across from me, I showed her my neck and told her my version of what had happened the night before. I referred to Andy as sick and violent. I could tell she wasn't convinced, but I left her no choice but to believe me.

I threw myself into work for the remainder of my summer. When a coworker offered me the use of her small house in Cape Cod, I seized the opportunity to disappear. Having heard tales of Provincetown, I wanted to investigate my conflicted sexuality and made my way there on the second day. It was summer and the beach was packed with men of every size and shape. I wondered if my skinny, pale body repulsed them. I kept my shirt on, as I was still underweight, but even my skinny legs made me feel shy. As I looked up, I saw a dark, curly-haired guy walking toward me.

"Are you alone? I'm Eddie."

I spent most of the next day exploring art galleries and walking the streets with him. He was kind and inquisitive without being intrusive. I was taken in by his good looks and New York accent, and guessed him to be in his late thirties. I was honest about my confusion but didn't tell him I had a girlfriend at home. He blamed a lot of my questioning on my age, which annoyed me. I felt older than my years and hated anyone suggesting I wasn't mature enough to handle any situation. The longer I stayed with him, the more electrified I felt when his hand grazed my arm or he leaned over to say something quietly in my ear. I had not spent this much time with a man I was sexually attracted to, and while I was nervous, I also felt exhilarated.

As the day wound down, he asked if we could take a walk on the beach. I put the butterflies in my stomach out of my mind and took his hand as he led me to a side street toward the bay. As he went down on me, he asked for nothing in return. He held me in a long embrace and walked me back to my car, handing me his number and telling me I was welcome to call him anytime if I needed to talk.

My head swirling with guilt and doubt, I went back to the cottage and searched for something to write on. Finding a package of envelopes, I poured out my heart and soul, writing out my worries and desires about how Eddie made me feel. I described the sexual experience with him in detail, and how it felt strange that he asked for nothing in return. I wrote questions I didn't know how to answer. I described my conflicts with Claudia and how I felt I was a freak and abnormal for having such deviant thoughts. I compared my sexual attraction to men versus women. The words poured out and filled envelope after envelope. When I finished, I contemplated burning them out of fear that someone would find them, but decided against it.

When I got back to Levittown, I had just a few short weeks until leaving for FIT. I spent the majority of that time with Claudia, and our relationship intensified, as did our sexual intimacy. Being with her made me feel more masculine. I felt worthy, and her desire for me was intoxicating. When we were together, I thought of nothing else and was able to keep out any thoughts of men or what I had done in Provincetown. Our fantasy continued with talk of marriage and running away. A part of me was grateful that the weeks passed quickly, before I had the chance to change my mind. Our goodbye was tearful, but inside I felt a spark of excitement. I understood the incredible opportunities I was facing, and made a promise to myself to explore every one of them.

I settled easily into dorm life, which surprised my doubting parents. Getting out of that house, away from them, was a freedom I had never experienced. To add to it, I was living in New York City with access to so many things to explore. I didn't waste any time searching out museums and exhibits and walking through the previews at Christie's and Sotheby's, fantasizing about the things I'd one day be able to collect. My classes inspired me, and I applied myself diligently to achieve good grades. I was amazed at what I was hearing and seeing, and started to see myself as an artistic person. When I spoke to my parents, I downplayed my excitement, sharing it only with Eileen. Every conversation with my father ended the same way: "When are you coming home?"

Claudia wrote me letters and sent me packages. I'd smile when I saw they were from her. I received a notice in my mailbox that there was a FedEx envelope for me, and was shocked to find hundreds of dollars in cash stuffed inside with a note reminding me to take good care of myself and to eat well. The cards that arrived shortly afterward, however, expressed a sadness I had not heard from her before. Our phone conversations grew tense, and I could feel her anger, which led to my frustration. I felt the weight of trying to maintain a relationship that I had accepted as doomed. I had my new life in the city ahead of me, and some part of her was coming undone.

I stopped hearing from her, and my letters went unanswered. Concerned, I tried contacting her at her parents' house, only to hear from her mother that Claudia was not well and I shouldn't call anymore. I attempted a few more letters, but they all went unanswered. The mystery intensified when the manager at Macy's contacted me, asking if I knew how to get in touch with her. She had months of paychecks that were not cashed. I knew I had to let her go, but my heart felt crushed.

I went back to Levittown to visit my parents as infrequently as my conscience would allow. When I did go, the routine was the same. I'd arrive at the train station, and my father would be there alone to pick me up. On the ride back to the house, he would talk to me about my mother: how her moods had been, what she was currently fixated on, and how lonely he felt. He did not ask about school. My mother would be happy enough to see me, and she would offer a hug and give her opinion on my appearance. It was never a warm homecoming unless Eileen came over. At least she would ask me about my life in the city. As we'd say goodnight, I lamented going upstairs to those bedrooms. Being back made me queasy, and I never slept soundly. Inevitably, I'd end up with a migraine, which I would nurse on the train ride back to Penn Station. My father's sadness was palpable when I left. He had a hard time looking at me and always asked when I'd be back again. My response was always the same, "Soon, Dad."

At the conclusion of my first year being away, I dreaded moving back home for the summer. I was distracted and felt a loathsome undercurrent as I packed my bags. My plan was to head home for the weekend and then return for final exams.

Focused on what lay in front of me, I didn't pause long enough to remember that the folder I stuffed into my duffle bag contained my journal of envelopes, the secrets my mother was about to discover.

PART II:
NEW YORK

Chapter Eight

The train ride back to New York City after that horrendous summer break was agonizing. I replayed the events and felt the humiliation of being called "faggot" by my mother all over again. She had joined the ranks of the high school bullies, stopping just short of spitting on me. My mother had always been unpredictable, so why was I surprised?

I tried to hate her, but I couldn't. This made me feel weak. It was not the first time I felt unloved by her, but this one hit me harder. She had rejected me.

I thought of all the things she had done to Eileen, my father, our family, and how I had no choice but to "forgive and forget," as my father repeatedly told us to do. But what did she mean when she said those words were for *him*, not me? Was she saying she thought he was gay? I couldn't shake the empty look in her eyes. I had witnessed her rage and sadness before, but this was different—darker, more remote. I vacillated between sadness, shame, anger, and concern. I wanted to be free of all these thoughts and feelings. Enough.

I was looking forward to a few weeks in the city before classes started again, and even had some money stashed away. My roommate had not gone home that summer, and knowing he would be there when I got back was at least a little reassuring.

The sudden darkness as we moved slowly through the tunnel startled me as I caught my reflection in the window. As I stared back and wondered what was wrong with me, I thought I might cry. I feared I might not be able to stop. I sat there with my shoulders hiked up to my ears and squeezed my hands together, keeping the tears locked up. I let out a big sigh as we pulled up to the platform and the conductor announced our arrival. When I emerged from Penn Station, the August sun hit me at once, and brought back the unpleasantness of New York in the stifling heat. Still, as I struggled with getting my bags into a cab, I started to really believe New York was now home.

Patrick, my roommate, had been out as a gay man for a long time. He was a few years older than me, and I appreciated his free spirit and "fuck it" attitude. After a hug, he pulled away and said, "Now it's time for a drink."

The Break was our local gay bar. It could be a little seedy, but I always felt safe there. We knew the bartenders and the regulars, and they let me drink without ever asking how old I was. My strategy was to order sophisticated drinks like Scotch or bourbon so they were less likely to be suspicious. Once established as a refined drinker, I could switch to something more affordable.

Scotch made my head swirl with cloudy memories of my father. That sting on my young lips as he put the glass to my mouth revisited me now, as I sat joking with Patrick. I smiled and pretended I had shaken off any lingering bad feelings from the preceding weeks. The longer I stayed there, glass in hand, the further away the thoughts of that summer went. I had discovered a harmless way of shutting things out. A hangover was a small price to pay for allowing myself to feel temporarily free from the things that polluted my thoughts.

As the fall semester started, I made a vow I would not fail. Failure of any kind represented vulnerability and weakness, qualities I now found intolerable in myself and in others. I also wanted to distance myself from my upbringing in Levittown. I needed to become someone else, someone who did not carry the stain of having come from where I did.

I believed Levittown was the source of the deep shame I struggled with.

I went home as infrequently as possible. During weekly check-in phone calls, my father acted as if nothing bad had ever happened. He spoke to me as if home was a place I must surely miss. My mother sounded sad. She told me she missed me, but it was difficult to trust her. She reminded me of the places I took her for special lunches and long drives in the country. She said things were not the same without me there, and she was lonely. I did not want to feel guilty, but I did. I told her I'd visit soon to spend the day with her, even bring her a present from New York.

I was not living under their roof, yet I still felt like their hostage.

My father was a champion at denying anything had ever gone wrong, and my mother continued to ask for unconditional love. When I tried to talk to Eileen, she reminded me I had no choice but to pretend it never happened. She had done that, and I must too, for the sake of our family. The thought infuriated me.

When I forced myself to go home for a visit, I'd inevitably wind up with debilitating migraines. They came on quickly and often left me curled up in bed with the curtains closed, blocking out any suggestions of light. My father blamed them on living in New York City. He told me in no uncertain terms I should be back home with them, and forget that disgusting place. This resulted in me trying to disguise when I had one. I'd take long showers, hoping the heat would help, and popped Excedrin like breath mints. These episodes left me feeling wrung out, and I'd sleep for the entire hour and a half train trip back to Penn Station.

Display and Exhibit Design was a two-year program. While I had hoped for a bachelor's degree, funds were already tight, and I needed to start earning money if I wanted to continue with my education. My father provided me with a credit card to use for the required art supplies, and he paid interest on the student loans I was accruing. Living expenses were up to me, a small price to pay for having gotten away from home.

I landed a job working in the Armani jeans department at Saks Fifth Avenue. It was a coveted position by students because the company provided you with the uniform: jeans and a white oxford or denim shirt. They also paid better than most of their competitors, and my retail background gave me an advantage. The hours were intense, amounting to just under full-time, but I knew I had to take on what they asked of me, or risk losing the job. Having made the dean's list the prior semester, I set a goal to maintain my grades for the remainder of my enrollment. I took honors classes and pushed myself to extremes, swallowing No-Doze tablets with a forty-ounce bottle of Budweiser to get me through the night.

I functioned in a muscle-knotted mess. After some trepidation, I decided to splurge on a massage. Patrick knew someone who worked close by, and was certain he could help me. I was nervous walking into the massage therapist's apartment, seeing the table and thinking it looked like an operating room.

The therapist was friendly and seemed confident as he approached me. Sensing my discomfort, he asked if this was my first massage and, if so, were there any areas that were particularly troubling. I talked about my tension, headaches, and stress level, and in return he assured me he knew exactly how to help.

My heart pounded when he instructed me to undress while he stepped out of the room to wash his hands. Undress? Does that mean underwear too or do I leave them on? Not knowing what to do, I left them on and crawled under the sheet, putting my face in the cradle. I hated being unclothed in front of people, especially men, always feeling self-conscious about my body.

As he got started, I relaxed under his hands, the thin cotton sheet protecting me from any direct contact. As he pulled it back, exposing my leg, he gently touched my hip and asked about my underwear. I explained I was unsure what to do, and thought I'd leave them on the first time. He again put me at ease by saying that I could do whatever felt comfortable. The tension started to escape my body. My emotions swirled, and I surrendered to the relaxation, feeling the pressure in my neck and behind my eyes fade.

I started to understand just how rigid I had been, and it made me sad. I wondered if it was normal to feel such things. When he asked me to turn over, I felt as though I was in a trance as he adjusted my body on the table, again laying the sheet softly over me. My head tingled as he worked intensely on my feet, and I sighed as points in my toes reverberated up through my sinuses. He moved his hands to my calves and knees, and I felt myself starting to get aroused. My face flushed, and I shifted under his hands, becoming aware of how uncomfortable I was.

The massage therapist kept working on my muscles and joints, and I wondered how he hadn't noticed what was happening under the sheet, under my underwear. Frustrated, I blurted out an apology and tried to sit up, wanting to conceal myself. He steadied his hand on my shoulder and told me it was a perfectly normal reaction and it was okay; however, it was not okay with me. I had gone from a state of relaxation I had never known to a feeling of exposed humiliation. I should have been able to prevent it from happening, but I had failed. I sat up and dropped my feet to the floor, covering myself.

"I need to leave. I'm really sorry." I pulled my clothes on quickly as he watched me. I handed him his fee and apologized again.

"I wish you'd stay. This happens all the time."

I didn't believe him. I left the building, attempting to look and feel normal. I needed to calm my nerves, to push this out of my mind. I walked down Eighth Avenue and into The Break, not wasting any time ordering multiple rounds of Scotch. By the time Patrick walked in, I was well on my way to being drunk. But this time, my nerves had not settled.

In my booze infused haze, I responded to Patrick's questions about the massage, how my day had been, and how my final project was coming along, with hostility and sarcasm. Alcohol usually softened my mood, but that night the anger I had been pushing down started to move up and out of me. As he tried to console me and ask what was wrong, I called him an asshole and blamed him for sending me to that creep massage therapist.

Patrick decided it was time to get me home, and as we walked up Eighth Avenue, I had a hard time maintaining my balance. As he came close to me to put his arm around my shoulders, I turned and unleashed a verbal assault that caused heads to turn. Giving in to my rage, I made a fist and half slapped, half punched him in the face. I was certain I had been victorious as he almost fell to the ground, but as he returned the blow, I stumbled and slipped off the curb, falling into Eighth Avenue. As he came over to help me stand, I pulled him down, wrapping my hands around his neck, trying to strangle him. I was covered in sweat and massage oil, saliva forming on my lips. He started laughing, which enraged me further, but I was no match for his sober stance. I screamed for him to leave me the fuck alone, and he did just that. I made it back to our dorm apartment hours later, where I found him soundly sleeping.

The next morning, I tried to make sense of what happened. I hated that I had lost my temper, and could hear my father's admonishment and criticism of my behavior as he called me Karen. I had acted just like her. I felt sick to my stomach and wanted to cry, but there was no time to let this get the better of me. I'd have to face Patrick in class that morning, as we all worked to finish our finals. I got to class late, and seeing him smirk as he and a group of friends laughed caused my face to burn. Trying to regain my footing, I worked quietly, but as he approached and asked if there was something I wanted to say to him, I erupted. I told him to fuck off and that he was a loser. He stood in front of me with the same smirk, not responding. I wanted to hit him again. Instead, I kicked a gallon of open paint across the room, ruining much of his work.

I had known this anger before. It felt familiar when I hit Patrick in the face. During one of my parents' violent feuds, Eileen and I raced downstairs to break them up for the third night in a row. We were exhausted and frustrated, and as I heard my mother scream at Eileen to go the fuck upstairs, anger took over. I was not yet eight years old, and I grabbed one of her brass bird statues from the corner table in the living room. I clenched it in my hands as I headed toward the garage. The idea of throwing it at her consumed me. I envisioned her shock and horror as she was covered in blood. Eileen, seeing what was happening, intercepted me and pried the statue out of my hands before anyone else noticed.

———

The department's final project was an art installation of hand-painted mannequins representing different eras. The exhibit was a moving tribute to what we learned during those two years. It also cemented my love for creating visual presentations. I had found a way to express myself without having to speak or reveal anything personal.

The day of the opening reception, I slammed back two vodkas at the bar before meeting my parents at the train station. They were intimidated by the city, and I dreaded them seeing me in creative surroundings. They didn't understand what the exhibit was about, but they were there, and that was an accomplishment in itself. When I pointed out the Keith Haring mannequin I had worked on, my mother's eyes filled with tears. I was on my third glass of cheap white wine and was moved by her reaction, so I went to hug her. I had misunderstood her emotion; she pulled away from me, creating an awkward distance.

"Are you an alcoholic?" she blurted out, a little too loudly.

I stared at her blankly. "No, Mom. I'm just having a good time."

"Be careful, Larry J. You don't want to end up like your uncle."

My face tingled. "I'm fine, Mom. Don't worry about me."

Allowing her to watch me drink freely was a mistake, and I felt ashamed for letting my guard down. I put them in a cab back to Penn Station and said my goodbyes. My father smiled, but looked lost as he tried to hold my mother's hand and she pushed him away. He had a long night ahead of him. I suspected I might be the subject of her discourse, and breathed a sigh of relief, knowing I wouldn't have any part in what unfolded between them on this night.

Graduation from FIT was held at Radio City Music Hall. It was a day I could only imagine just a few years earlier. I felt an incredible sense of pride, having made the dean's list three out of four semesters, and as a result, graduating Magna Cum Laude. I stayed away from any alcohol that day to avoid stares and comments from my mother, and tried to keep the celebration afterward brief, enjoying a short meal before sending them home.

Eileen beamed as she reminded me she always knew I'd succeed. I loved having her there. She had sent me cards, care packages, and spending money during my two years and was my most loyal friend. In return, I loved sharing all the fun and fascination of New York City with her, and when she visited, we'd go to movies, museums, and cafés in Soho.

I struggled with what was next for me, but kept those fears to myself.

Penny, who had encouraged me to enroll at FIT, and I decided to get an apartment together. It was a way to navigate a difficult city with little money. The apartment we found was in Times Square, at a time when it was still gritty. We shared a one-bedroom on the second floor just above Café Un Deux Trois on West Forty-Fourth Street. We decorated our apartment in an eccentric bohemian style, with mirrors lining the walls, a makeshift second bedroom in the living area, and faux gilded furniture. Our personal style of dress reflected our apartment. Penny in chunky knit sweaters and tight pants, and me in printed polyester shirts with loose fitting pants. By now, I had discovered a way to conceal my ears. I grew my hair down to my shoulders, and developed my own look: part John Lennon and part Jesus of Nazareth. Finally mature enough to need to shave, I experimented with facial hair, sporting an on-again off-again goatee in an attempt to embrace a more masculine appearance.

We went to jazz clubs on Restaurant Row and dive bars in the East Village. We cohabitated with roaches that oozed from our kitchen cabinets and mice that made their way upstairs from the restaurant below—defiant, determined mice that did not scurry away even as we let out deafening screams. We had no money, but our lives were rich with adventure.

I'd scour the job placement board at FIT and then head to The Break for a drink before walking back to Times Square. It was a way to celebrate a new job prospect, or lament the fact that there was nothing worth pursuing. A drink was the answer for either scenario.

On a day I was feeling optimistic, I ordered a Scotch and was surprised and relieved to hear that a guy at the end of the bar paid for it. I had seen Anthony before. He was about a decade older than me, Italian with a full head of black hair, pronounced features, and a solid muscular form. The hair on his chest was always visible from his white button-down shirts, and his jeans were always a little too tight. I raised my glass and smiled, which brought him down to sit next to me. After making small talk, he wasted no time in asking me back to his apartment. Afternoon free and feeling adventurous, I agreed.

Anthony's apartment was messy, but I barely had time to notice before he ushered me to his bed. As we started to kiss, I sensed his impatience as he navigated himself from being under me to on top of me. He was heavy to begin with, but as he aggressively pushed himself further onto me, I found it hard to breathe. As he fumbled with his jeans, my chest started to tighten. He was more excited than I had experienced in a man before, and as he thrust himself down onto my stomach, he buried me under his weight and covered my mouth with his. I felt dizzy and nauseated and pushed at his shoulders, but I was no match for his sexual aggression. He eagerly ejaculated on my stomach and then collapsed on top of me. I closed my eyes and tried to focus, feeling paralyzed under him. I felt like screaming, but couldn't understand why.

After what seemed like an eternity, he lifted his head from being nestled against my neck, and rolled to one side. "Sorry buddy. Am I too heavy?"

Still not able to speak, I shifted and tried to free my legs from the entanglement of his. I got to the side of the bed and stood, buttoning my shirt.

"Want me to finish you off before you go?" I shook my head and without saying anything, walked to the door.

"See you again?"

I lied, "Yeah, sure."

Out on the street, I felt panicked. I thought of that time with Andy back at home. My head started to pound, and my hands shook with fear. I needed this last hour erased from my mind before I went crazy. I got myself back to the apartment and polished off what was left of a bottle of vodka. It wasn't enough. I went to the closest bar and drank myself into a stupor, making it home in time to spend the rest of the night violently throwing up. That gave me something else to focus on, and pushed out my distasteful memories.

Debilitated by an awful hangover, I decided to stay away from bars and excessive drinking for a while, and focus on finding a job.

I avoided speaking to my father. I didn't want to hear his doubts about my ability to find work and have him try to convince me to come home. Since graduating, I hardly heard from my mother. Eileen told me she was consumed with the health of her poodle, and spent every day carrying him around and nurturing him. I appreciated this explanation, but inside I knew she had distanced herself from me. It was her way of punishing me for leaving her behind. Our role reversal left me frustrated and sad at the same time. I dreamt of a mother I could turn to, one who would embrace a son who loved her unconditionally. If I didn't make an effort to call her, we could go weeks without speaking. I was hurt, but didn't want to admit it to her or myself.

I found some freelance work through my friend Charles, and got by for a while doing a gold-leaf stenciling job for a wealthy family on the Upper West Side. I lost myself in that work, spending hours adding beauty to an already impeccable example of architecture. I spent my evenings with Penny, drinking tea and listening to music. We were not ideal roommates by any means, but we relied on each other in a city that could leave you feeling both decimated and exhilarated on the same day.

After months of no hope for a steady job, a new posting appeared, from a textile company looking for a visual merchandiser. The salary was low by New York standards, but I was starting to feel desperate and thought I should at least go on the interview. A few weeks later, I found myself sitting at a desk at Fabric Traditions, a company that sold printed cottons to the home sewing industry. I hated the product, but was more than ready to feel the security of a nine-to-five job that came with benefits and a travel schedule that promised to get me away on a regular basis. I had not traveled much and looked forward to new destinations, even the less-than-desirable places like Tupelo, Bentonville, and Amarillo. The break from Penny and the growing tension between us also appealed to me. Needing to recover financially from months of not working, I walked ten blocks home every day at lunch to eat cans of tuna and sardines that I bought from a dollar store.

Fabric Traditions was a conservative environment, and I felt like a fish out of water. I kept my life private and shared little with my bosses and coworkers. The surroundings added to my feelings of confusion, and I imagined what it must feel like to be confident and secure. I was neither but could fake it, a skill that would clearly be necessary if I was going to last at this job.

My relationship with Penny fractured. She had fallen in love with a guy who we allowed to move in with us, thinking the extra rent contribution would help. It was a bad idea from the beginning. My resentment grew to an unmanageable level. The three of us went from moments of feeling like family and sharing meals together to having a fight that caused an awkward silence lasting for days.

I complained bitterly to a coworker while away on a business trip. As I was regaling her with my tales of domestic unrest, she told me she might have a solution. Rent-controlled apartments were hard to come by in New York. Her boyfriend was moving in with her, and he had his sister's studio on the Upper East Side. With any luck, I might be able to land the apartment. After a few nail-biting weeks, I received word that the lease would be transferred to my name. I had to come up with the money for the security deposit, which I did by withdrawing cash on my credit card over a few days, and had to agree to accept the apartment in "as is" condition. I was willing to do anything. Not only was I getting out of the bad situation with Penny, but also scoring a studio apartment on my own. It was the moment of independence I had hoped for. Without regret, Penny and I parted ways as roommates and our friendship ended.

The apartment measured about twelve by twelve, with a tiny kitchen area and ample bathroom. It smelled of a gas leak, had a crumbling wall, and the appliances were older than I was. Still, I loved it and was thrilled to call it home. I was in my element creating order out of chaos, and this was no exception.

The whole apartment was not much larger than my room at home, but now, I was paying eight-hundred dollars a month, and the only screaming I heard was an occasional bone-chilling screech from the aspiring opera singer one flight down. From the top floor of a four-story tenement, I had a sweet view of the small garden apartments nestled behind the neighboring buildings. On rainy days, I'd pull a chair up to the window and dream what my life could become if I worked hard and played my cards right.

Eileen shared in my excitement, but my parents remained silent. When I told Eileen I was disappointed they didn't call to congratulate me on my new apartment, Eileen simply said, "You know Mom. She's feeling sorry for herself."

Days later when my mother did call, I boldly said I had hoped to hear from her sooner. Changing her tone, she admonished me for acting spoiled and telling her what to do. She reminded me she was my *mother*, and it was not my place to question her, instead I only needed to love her. She went on to ask me if I understood how difficult it was being left alone with just "him," and how hard it was without her little boy there to make her laugh, buy her presents, and help her feel good about herself.

"You're the only one that can do that, Larry J., and you left me." Breaking down into sobs, she said she had to hang up.

After conversations with my parents, I used alcohol to combat the anxiety I felt. Getting out of the apartment offered me a reprieve, so I headed straight to my favorite local bar. One night, I noticed a man sitting alone in the corner. When he looked my way, I managed a smile and when he smirked shyly back, I took a chance and sat down next to him, my need to fully escape consuming me.

James was a tall, fair-haired man with a sweet smile and glasses. His timid demeanor and subtle good looks took me by surprise, as I usually found myself drawn to more assertive men. I wanted to go home with him, but he resisted, giving me his number instead and saying he'd like to see me again. This was new territory for me, but I thought it was time to try something fresh. Instead of immediately falling into bed and ending things by the time I left, I decided to let this situation play out.

I had never been on an actual date with a man before. I told myself I wanted more than quick hookups, but I repeated the same behavior over and over again. I believed if I developed feelings for a man, it would lead to nothing but hurt and shame. Would I lose my parents forever? Did I then deserve to be called a faggot? My conflict in being attracted to men became something I had to control. That attraction superseded any desire to pursue sex with women, yet I wasn't ready to close that door entirely.

When I met James at a Chinese restaurant for dinner, we had a great time, which surprised me, and it left me wanting to see him again. On our second date, he invited me to his apartment, where we talked and slowly got to know each other better. He worked as a park ranger, his territory covering Ellis and Liberty Islands. His work fascinated me, and the idea of dating a park ranger in New York City was exciting.

We were lustful for each other before becoming sexual. I was flooded with anticipation before every encounter, and to add to the intrigue, he took me on adventures. We went on ten-mile walks along the Hudson River, through small towns and aqueduct trails, stopping for lunch and talking about history. He brought me to Brooklyn's Prospect Park and described its plan in great detail, explaining to me why he believed it was superior to Central Park. On these excursions, we had moments of tenderness and affection that caught me off guard, as the butterflies in my stomach took over and danced around, making me feel woozy with excitement.

James never pressured me sexually. He followed my lead and was content with being physical and sexual on my terms. I was not interested in anal sex, which only reaffirmed my belief that I must not be gay. My one attempt at anal sex with a man ended in disaster, when I stopped abruptly and insisted we were finished. It wasn't an issue with James. He excited me *and* made me feel safe. His firm hugs were often a welcome place to retreat to when I was privately concerned about money, family, or work.

On a beautiful spring day, I took off work to spend time with James. He had a surprise for me, but said it would require a few hours of my time and a weekday would be preferable. My instructions were to meet him at his apartment by eight o'clock on the morning of our appointed day. We hopped on the subway, and on the way downtown, he laughed as he said that he was taking me to work with him. I cringed as I remembered going to work with my father, but tried to keep my focus on James and his thoughtfulness. I had never been to the Statue of Liberty or Ellis Island, and that's where he was taking me. He responded to my enthusiasm with a smile that gave me chills. No one had ever looked at me the way he did, and I basked in how good it felt.

The ferry across the Hudson River to the Statue of Liberty was enough to make me happy. Once we arrived at the port, there was no waiting in line or admission to pay. James ushered me through a separate door and into the secluded hallways of the behind-the-scenes offices. He introduced me to his coworkers as we passed them, and feeling shy, I mostly just smiled. Waiting for him, I wandered the halls, mesmerized by the beauty of the building. I felt his hands on my shoulders and leaned into him as he said softly, "Let's start the real tour."

From the top of the Statue of Liberty, he pointed out landmarks and directed my eyes and attention to the lesser-known points of interests. I was fascinated hearing him say there was housing for the park rangers on Liberty Island. Pointing, he said some of his friends lived in small houses just beyond a row of evergreens.

As we headed back to Ellis Island, he told me to follow him as we walked toward a blocked-off section that was masked by trees. I was transfixed as we came upon enormous, unrenovated buildings hidden from public view. These buildings were originally used for infirmed immigrants and contained offices and hospital facilities. The long, brick hallways were lined with arched metal-framed windows, many of them opened slightly as if someone needed fresh air. There were rooms with abandoned desks, chairs still in place, and paint crumbling from the walls and ceilings. Kitchen facilities had old tiled walls and counters that were still intact, and strange-looking furnaces or incinerators with their doors left open. Light filtered in through the vines and overgrowth that covered the exterior, and as James filled my head with stories, I hung on his every word, taking it all in.

Leading me down a long passageway, he pushed open a wood door barely attached to its hinges. He took my hand as we stepped outside to sit down, close to the water's edge. He asked if I was having a good time. With a smile I couldn't mask, I said yes before leaning in to kiss him. Pulling me in closer, we remained there for a long time, caught up in our affection. I loved being close to him, and as he whispered those unforgettable words in my ear, I knew I loved him too.

———

At Saks, I worked with an openly gay man who reminded me of my mother, when she was fun. Jake was youthful and needy. He collected stuffed animals and was obsessed with Disney World and its characters. He and I often went out drinking after work and could laugh and carry on until the wee hours. Nothing was ever too heavy with him, and I welcomed that escape from the anxiety I usually carried. We stayed in touch after I quit, but didn't see each other as often. When he called to ask me to meet him at the diner and not at a bar, I had a moment of worry I tried to dismiss. But as I walked in and saw him sitting there, eyes swollen, and looking troubled, I knew something was wrong.

"Hi, Mary," he said, trying to sound upbeat, calling me by his favorite nickname.

I didn't waste any time. "What's wrong?"

For the next hour I listened intently as he explained he had contracted HIV. As he sobbed, he pleaded with me to still be his friend. I held his hand and reassured him he could count on me, that this didn't change anything in terms of our friendship. We pulled ourselves together and decided the best thing to do was to get drunk. Seeing him slam back martinis in quick succession, I chose to take it slow myself. With help, I got him into a cab and home.

Jake's news unsettled me. He had asked that I keep it quiet, which I did, but I found myself consumed with worry. Though my sexual activity had been limited, now I feared that by some fluke, I might have contracted HIV through kissing or oral sex. I anxiously recounted the men I had been with. Had I come into contact with semen? Did jerking off with a guy and having him ejaculate on me put me at risk? Obsessive research put my mind at ease but only temporarily. I continued to fear that I might be HIV positive; however, I remained silent about my concerns.

I pulled away from James without explanation. I heard disappointment and confusion in his voice when he called, but I left his messages unanswered. I told myself if I continued pursuing men, it was inevitable that I too would become HIV positive.

The only choice was to put attraction and feelings for men out of my mind and body forever. James was a casualty of that decision.

In addition to his freelance creative work, Charles also played bass in a small band that performed in the city's obscure music venues. I was loyal to his various pursuits and rarely missed one of his gigs. I liked the crowds that gathered at these places, mostly straight but with an undertone of openness and curiosity. I felt at ease in these surroundings. I started to spend more time with him and his girlfriend, hoping to put James out of my thoughts.

Their wide array of friends, most of them significantly older than me, was made up of writers, musicians, and artists. They reminded me of the thespians and musicians in high school, but now there were no bullies to be wary of, and I was accepted for being me. It was the first time I felt safe saying I was bisexual. It was a label I felt I could live with, in light of my confusing thoughts.

After one of his performances far downtown, Charles came over to greet me with a big hug. He turned to kiss his girlfriend, and then interrupted her as she spoke to another woman. Beaming with excitement, he turned back toward me with a wink and asked, "Oh hey, have you met Katherine?"

Chapter Nine

Katherine, nine years my senior, was a freelance writer. I was somewhat intimidated by her, but she put me at ease with her calm energy and wicked sense of humor. My mind stayed on our meeting in that dark club after Charles's gig; it was easy to recall her features. She was tall, with dark hair cut like Mia Farrow's in *Rosemary's Baby,* giving her a boyish appearance. Her body was fit, and she moved through the room with a steady grace that kept my attention. But what had me thinking about her as I settled into bed were her eyes. She had the most beautiful, large, doe-like pair I had ever seen. I felt I could gauge people by whether or not they made eye contact. Not only did her eyes meet mine, they steadied themselves on me and seemed to see into me.

I knew I'd be seeing Katherine at Charles's next show, and in preparation I decided to get my hair cut, buy a new outfit that made me look a little older, and attempt to make a good impression. Charles teased me about my hair, calling me a little elf, but Katherine, taking my arm, whispered in my ear that she thought I looked adorable, and as she kissed me on the cheek, I was reminded of the excitement I felt on my first date with Claudia.

We started seeing each other without the accompaniment of our mutual friends. We met for tea and spent afternoons walking through Manhattan. The first time I invited her to my apartment, I worried she would think it was too feminine. I had worked hard at developing my own aesthetic, achieving a look that spoke of weathered English farmhouses and decrepit manors. Taking precautions, I tucked away vases, throw pillows, and antique transferware dishes, quickly realizing I'd have to empty the entire contents to not give away the proclivities of the man who inhabited it. Instead, she embraced it wholeheartedly, the same way she had embraced my hair and my youth. Age was not an issue for either of us. There was a timeless quality to our conversations. We spent many hours in my apartment, and our conversations moved fluidly. When our affections turned more passionate, I knew an honest and uncomfortable heart-to-heart talk was on the horizon.

I confessed I had experimented sexually with men, and exaggerated my experiences with women. I felt too embarrassed to admit I had only slept with one woman, three years ago. I was nervous speaking about my attraction to men, and avoided her eyes.

Katherine looked at me with a smile and said, "Isn't everyone at least a little gay?"

It was another moment of appreciating just how different she was. Fearing judgment, I received the ultimate acceptance instead. This was new to me, a far cry from my experience with my parents. I felt protective of my vulnerability, but I let her into my heart.

I understood what I was doing. I was turning a blind eye and making a decision to start over, denying the fact that I was gay. My fears and doubts exploded with Jake's HIV diagnosis, and I believed I was safer in a heterosexual relationship. But I also knew there would be challenges. As we walked around the city arm in arm, I feared I would run into a man I had slept with or had known from a gay bar. I felt self-conscious about my mannerisms and became vigilant in acting straight, not crossing my legs and attempting to keep my voice from too high a pitch. Relieved to be physically attracted to her, I was convinced I'd have no trouble performing in bed. I had a righteous determination to prove this was my intended fate.

I dreaded getting an HIV test, a burdensome obstacle before going any further with Katherine. My stomach churned with worry as I researched anonymous clinics in the city. I confided in Jake that I had decided to pursue a relationship with a woman. He laughed as he called me Mary and made jokes at my expense, telling me I would miss men in no time. He was the only person I trusted enough to tell I was getting tested. He tried to reassure me that based on my experience, I had nothing to worry about.

I believed that if I were indeed HIV positive, I deserved it. It would be my punishment for giving in to a desire that I didn't fully understand or accept. I made a list of all the men I had slept with and rated my risk factors. I had received plenty of blowjobs but had given few. The fact that I had never swallowed eased my worry, but that was short-lived, as I became consumed with statistics. I could be in the minority, contracting it through deep kissing or contact with semen on my hands or body. By the time I actually went in for the test, I was shaking with anxiety.

In the early nineties there was a three-day waiting period for results. As time ticked along, I kept my fears and shame to myself, bottling everything up into a tight knot. Hearing the nurse tell me that my results were negative, I leapt up and thanked her. She handed me a brochure on how to practice safer sex and advised me to get checked every six months. My thoughts were elsewhere, as the last obstacle to moving forward with Katherine had cleared.

From here on out, I'd be a new man.

Katherine and I dated for weeks before sleeping together. She didn't drink, which resulted in me drinking significantly less. Not losing myself in mind-numbing alcohol increased my desire for sex. As I pushed, incessantly at times, she continued to hold me at bay. My experiences had mostly been quick and impulsive. I was not used to waiting or allowing tension to build. I stayed aroused all night when we had platonic sleepovers, but remained patient, trusting she would indulge me when she was ready. The nurturing and respect we provided one another filled my heart, and I felt lost in the hours we were apart. I had fallen in love with this woman who cared deeply for me. We expressed ourselves through letters, long conversations, and a connection that only grew with time.

I had not had much experience using condoms. I bought a box in anticipation of our first lovemaking adventure, but I worried about how things would go. On a trial run, alone in my apartment, my concerns were validated as I struggled to maintain my erection while trying to unroll the thin covering onto my penis. Feeling defeated, I decided to wait and see what happened in that critical moment, hoping it wouldn't be a disaster.

When an evening turned undeniably erotic, I tried moving myself closer to her unprotected. Pulling her face back, she looked at me and said, "You need a jacket." She laughed as I rolled my eyes and reached under my bed to grab one of the condoms I had strategically placed there. I fumbled with the wrapping, but I was exhilarated when I had no trouble with the assembly. As I moved inside of her, I was once again flooded with that feeling of being normal. That same welcoming sensation of losing my virginity came back, and I believed this was what sex should feel like.

We had sex as often as we could. In my mind, the traditional position, man on top, was ideal. I loved feeling wanted and needed, and when our bodies connected this way, my self-esteem inflated. I felt powerful having her nails claw into my back, and my uneasiness about my skinny body disappeared. My narrow frame moved effortlessly on top of her, and the resulting bruises on her inner thighs from my hips were reminders of the pleasure we had shared.

Oral sex with a woman was new to me, but I quickly discovered it was not something I enjoyed. Realizing I would have to do it for her pleasure, I would only engage in it after heavy drinking, hoping she'd never realize the coincidence. An all fours position reminded me of the men that asked me to fuck them and made me cringe. One failed attempt in that configuration with her put an end to it as I fumbled and started in on the wrong point of entry. It was an awkward moment— one that in my humiliation I tried to laugh off, knowing I'd better never try again. I never imagined this kind of connection to another human, and the fact that I had never found this with a man reinforced my determination to remain loyal to her.

Katherine was the most accepting and loving person I had ever experienced. Her patience and kindness to others was inspiring. I knew my parents were going to love her, and that had me conflicted. The anger that moved through me, out of reach, told me they didn't deserve to enjoy the life I was creating. On the flip side, I still hoped my mother would find a way to love and embrace me. I believed that now, with Katherine completing the picture, it might just be within reach. When it came to my father, I was relinquishing control, knowing he was going to feel he'd gotten his way, and we'd be a big, happy family. I wondered how the first introduction would go. Would my mother cry with happiness because I brought a girl home? Would my father tell her stories about when I was a kid? I prepared to be embarrassed by whatever they might say.

Katherine immediately embraced my parents. She could joke around with my father and knew just how to coddle my mother. She arrived with presents and hugs and didn't mind sitting in front of the television with them. There was no mention of my sexuality except for my father whispering, after embracing me just a little too long, "I'm glad that other bullshit is behind you now."

Visits home were far more tolerable with her at my side, and I even made it through Christmas. Piles of meaningless gifts were laid out for us. Through tears, my mother confessed she loved "Kate," and she was so happy I brought her into their lives. Every time we visited, my father thanked her for bringing his son back to him. Now when my migraines set in, Katherine helped me to bed, loaded with Excedrin, and kissed me on the forehead, a reminder I would be okay.

On the major things, Katherine and I agreed. I moved into her apartment without incident, and she allowed me to make any changes I felt necessary. She helped me find a tenant to sublet my studio, and we declared ourselves officially living together. Marriage wasn't necessary, and neither of us wanted children. The idea of having a child felt out of reach to me and would only muddle my already confused mind. This took a lot of pressure off, and we were relieved to not dwell on such things.

While I avoided going home without Katherine, I took an opportunity to visit Eileen and celebrate the news of her pregnancy. The train was crowded, and a person attempting to store bags overhead annoyed me. As I looked up, a tall, handsome man stared back. I smirked and immediately looked down, feeling like I had just been caught doing something wrong. Feeling his gaze on me made my face flush. I closed my eyes and was filled with the quick snapshots I had seen—his crooked collar grazing his tanned skin, the dark scruff covering his chin, and his piercing eyes. From near the exit, he smiled and motioned with a nod for me to come over to him. Feeling excited and self-conscious simultaneously, I maneuvered past the woman sitting next to me. As I got closer, I realized just how well built he was, and my body tingled with nervous excitement. I was not accustomed to men this attractive noticing me, and I let my ego take over, coupled with the stir I felt in my jeans just by looking at him.

We made small talk about the packed train, destinations, and him missing his stop, at which point he said, "I almost didn't stay on the train, thinking you probably have a boyfriend or even a girlfriend."

I blurted out honestly, "I do."

His expression shifted to one of annoyance and disgust as he told me what he thought of me. Turning, he faced the door waiting for the train to stop, and he abruptly got off. I quietly made my way back to my seat, hoping no one saw what just transpired. I was filled with shame and felt stained. As far as I was concerned, I had just been caught doing something horrible. I had difficulty acknowledging I still found men attractive and loved being noticed by them.

When making love to Katherine, I trained myself to think only of our mutual physical pleasure. The sensation was enough to keep my focus on enjoying the intensity between our bodies. But when I wasn't engaged in sex with her, my thoughts wandered to images of men, memories of those I had been with and fantasies of others I had yet to encounter.

Not long after my train debacle, I retrieved a voice mail message from James at work. The urgency in his voice was unnerving, and he asked that I meet with him. When I called him back, that same anxious tone remained as he told me there was something he needed to tell me.

My heart raced as I made my way over to the diner a few blocks away from my office, and sweat collected on my back and temples. I had blocked him out of my thoughts since meeting Katherine but was now forced to revisit the guilt I felt for ending things the way I had. He was sitting in a booth, and our eyes met as I walked in. I instantly regretted being there. Seeing his sad face flooded my senses, and I wanted to hug him and tell him I was sorry. But it was too late. As I sat down, he told me how badly I had hurt him, and that he needed me to know he was in love with me.

I held my composure and said calmly, "James, I'm so sorry, but I have fallen in love with a woman."

His expression turned to anger. He stood and yelled at me, "You are gay, Larry. Accept it! You're making a huge mistake."

As he stormed out, I sat frozen with humiliation, not knowing what to do. That night I arrived home with flowers and dinner. I made Katherine a special picnic that we enjoyed by candlelight out on the balcony and ended our evening by making love slowly and tenderly. I needed to convince myself I had embraced this life honestly and without question; James was wrong about me.

After a challenging pregnancy, Eileen gave birth to my perfectly healthy niece, Charlotte. She was something new and exciting to talk about.

With some hesitation, Eileen gave in to my parents' suggestion that my mother provide daycare for Charlotte, the argument being it would keep my mother occupied and provide them much-needed extra income. Just the right dose of guilt sealed the deal with Eileen. She would not refuse them. I wondered how she could possibly trust my mother and struggled to understand her rationalization. When I spoke to my father, I learned how much pressure he had put on her. Eileen's reservations were no match for his own needs. My biggest fear was our mother simply deciding one day she no longer wanted this "job," leaving Eileen stranded. No negotiation with my parents involved bargaining; it was only about being compliant with what they wanted.

———

In the spring, our musician friend Charles was accepted into a writing retreat in Scotland. Katherine and I wanted to travel to Paris, and impulsively, we decided to do it. We'd start our adventure in Edinburgh, spend a night in London, and cross the tunnel on the train to spend a few days in Paris.

I also had further plans. I felt desperate to tame what I considered a continuing unhealthy attraction to men. In my restless state, I resorted to what I had always done: take action for the sake of taking action. It was a way to avoid dealing with the truth that simmered under the surface. While in Paris, I'd ask her to marry me, in turn sealing our fate as a committed and monogamous couple. I tried to convince myself that by getting married, I would settle down and keep my desires and turgid thoughts from emerging. My desperation overruled any questions about the lasting effects of my plan. I reminded myself those endless hookups left me feeling empty, and convinced myself I had a problem.

Eileen was the only person I told of my plans. I left the antique store on Tenth Street where I had just picked up a tiny, silver, antique diamond ring. It was simple, yet the perfect gesture for this classic woman whom I considered my best friend. Eileen's reaction was tepid.

"Are you sure?"

She caught me off guard, and within seconds, I found myself trying to convince both of us this was such a good idea. I spoke of love, commitment, security, future, and finally said, "I don't want to be alone, and I'm afraid that's what could happen."

In my most conflicted emotional moments I could say anything to Eileen, and she listened without criticism. As we hung up the phone, she said she just wanted to see me happy. If marrying Katherine would do that, I had her blessing. I thanked her, and asked her to wish me luck.

I did not speak any French, but Katherine could fake it well enough. Paris struck us both instantly; the people, the food, and the visual stimulation surrounded and lured us in. We were enthralled and held each other closely as we explored the streets. We exhausted ourselves by walking miles each day and turned in early to our tiny hotel room, with its worn chintz wallpaper and a bed barely large enough to accommodate us lying side by side.

On our second day, I suggested we walk to the Tuileries Gardens. I slipped the ring into my pocket from its hiding place inside one of my socks and nervously fumbled with it. My body tightened and my stomach grumbled as we followed the signs directing us to the famous park. Finding a bench, I suggested we sit for a while. I turned to her and attempted to speak, stammering.

"Larry, what is it?" she asked, genuinely concerned.

I pulled my thoughts together in an instant, and I said, "I know we both said this wasn't important, but I have changed my mind and I'm hoping you will too. Will you marry me?"

Her look of astonishment surprised me. Deep down I assumed she knew this was coming. With tears in her eyes, she hugged me and whispered yes, but privately I sensed her hesitation.

When we got home, Eileen and her husband came into the city to celebrate our engagement, leaving Charlotte in the care of my parents for her first overnight stay. Eileen was relaxed, on a break from mothering a colicky baby, and I was happy to have some time with my sister. Our phone rang, and Katherine answered it, then called me into the kitchen, whispering with a concerned look, "It's your dad."

After his standard, "Hello, Son," he said my mother wasn't acting right.

"What do you mean, not right?" I asked, instantly frustrated, since this was nothing new.

"I don't know. She's slurring her words and won't get up from the chair. I thought she was drunk, but she got pissed at me for asking, and now won't speak to me."

This was out of character. If she were drinking, she'd be irate by now. I asked to speak to her, but as I heard him say her name repeatedly, I could tell that something bad had happened.

"Mom? Are you okay?"

It was obvious she couldn't speak, as I heard crying and garbled mumbling. My father got back on the phone. Putting the pieces together, I asked him the looming question, "How's her face?"

Sounding annoyed at my inquisition, he told me the side of her face was slouched, confirming my fears that she had suffered a stroke. I urged him to call an ambulance, and we all got into a cab to Penn Station. I called again before we got on the train, and he told me they would wait for us to get there.

"Dad, you need to get her to the hospital now."

He hesitated, then said, "She won't go without you."

After we got her checked in, the doctor told us she was lucky she did not have another stroke or worse yet, die. I grilled my father on what transpired and was horrified to learn she had fallen the night before and couldn't stand on her own. She had gone close to twenty-four hours untreated.

In her room, I cried, hugging her, telling her how happy I was she was okay, and at the same time, I was furious at my father. I struggled to understand how he could've watched this unfold and not done anything. It brought back my childhood, their vicious fighting, the danger Eileen and I constantly faced, and his oblivious neediness. I had a hard time being in the same room with him and avoided looking at him, silent as the anger whirled inside of me.

I took the following week off from work and stayed there long enough to see her released from the hospital and settled. After running countless tests, they didn't come to any conclusion as to why this happened to my young, fifty-year-old mother. She was given a low fat, low sodium diet, and I watched my father roll his eyes and mumble out loud that it wouldn't last.

The stroke left its mark on her speech, but she and I discovered she could sing without any noticeable impediment. Fascinated, we sang nursery rhymes. She looked directly at me when we did this, and her laughter turned to tears as she hugged me, thanking me for being with her.

As the week came to an end, my mother was despondent as I got ready to head back to New York. I prepared healthy meals and stocked the freezer. Out of earshot, I pleaded with my father to make sure she did her physical therapy. Even as I said it, I knew it was unlikely, but I attempted to feel as if I had some control over what would happen when I left them alone.

When I called to check on her, I heard my father's frustration as he asked how soon I'd be back. I returned the following weekend. As I walked into the house, I was horrified to see the garbage can filled with pizza boxes and fast food bags. Livid, I asked him what was going on, after seeing the freezer contents untouched.

"If you're not here, I can't promise anything. She won't listen to me."

Feeling defeated, I opted to take them to her favorite diner, thinking I could show them how to eat out and still follow her diet.

My father laughed as he said, "As long as you're paying, we'll do it,"

This caused my mother to laugh along for the first time since my return. When I told her she could have dessert, her eyes lit up like a gratified child. My attempts to have her get the fruit plate were ignored, as she dove into chocolate cake with ice cream. I indulged in rice pudding, seeking out my own form of comfort after a challenging day. I stared down as I focused my attention on the soft grains melting in my mouth. I swirled the cinnamon with my spoon, surprised to find a whole cinnamon stick in my diner-style rice pudding. I nudged it around further, ignoring them.

"Stop playing with your food," my father snapped, shaking me back to reality.

As I regained awareness of my surroundings, I saw it wasn't a stick of cinnamon, but rather a huge cockroach. Disgusted and nauseated, I took this as an omen: it was time to say my farewells and head back to New York.

I visited my mother less frequently, which felt like the right decision for my peace of mind, but filled me with guilt about leaving her alone with my father. I sent her care packages and called often to ask if she was doing her exercises. I knew she was lying to me, and when I pressed her on it, she cried, saying they hurt, she was bored, and there was no point in doing them. I found myself offering her an incentive. For every ten minutes she spent doing her therapy, I would send her ten dollars. I was too embarrassed to tell Katherine what I had done. I started posting cash the following day, wanting my mother to take it seriously. The deal ended when I neglected to send payment fast enough. I asked her to please continue, but she was adamant.

"No. You ruined your chance. Keep your ten dollars."

I became short-tempered and felt fragile. The evidence appeared on my cheeks, in the form of a deep red color that took over as my heart raced. I felt the craving for complete distraction and the numbing effects of alcohol, but Katherine kept me grounded and watched me closely. She saw I was not in a good state of mind, and she did everything possible to be supportive.

I became impatient discussing our wedding plans. What had started out as a small intimate gathering of a few friends and immediate family now included cousins, aunts, and people I had never heard of. I wanted to marry my best friend, which I was sure would fix me, but I was facing regurgitated feelings, and as my fears intensified, so did my intolerance.

Katherine knew and understood me like no other. She felt it too, and over a course of months, we sank into acceptance that we might be losing one another. The future of our marriage and relationship as lovers came into an undeniable light when I failed to get aroused. My head rushed with memories of my father's erection problems and my mother's resulting admonishment. I felt like him, and was consumed with a raw self-hate. The only thing to shake me out of the disgust was when Katherine leaned over, kissed me on the forehead, and said she loved me.

That was the difference. I wasn't him, and she was not my mother. I was safe even in the uncertainty of what was to come.

Things were increasingly unstable in Levittown. I heard from Eileen and my father that my mother was having trouble sleeping, and that she was even more irrational. On a visit home, I could see she looked irritated, preoccupied. She insisted that at night, she could hear the neighbors talking about her. Eileen and my father told her she was crazy. As a result, her anger toward them intensified, along with her distrust. On my visit, she called me upstairs to my old room, pointing toward the window.

Placing her ear against the screen, she whispered, "Listen. Do you hear that?"

Hearing nothing, I answered, "Yes, Mommy. I hear it."

I was instinctively aware when my mother needed reassuring and felt no conflict about lying to her in that moment. It was essential to gain her trust.

She took my hand, which surprised me, and added, "Those assholes downstairs think I'm crazy."

I worried about her as I returned to New York.

Katherine and I agreed to keep our impending break up quiet until we sorted out the logistics. I planned on breaking the news to my parents over Easter dinner, with Eileen there for moral support. I was distraught, trusting Eileen to help steady me.

Eileen had warned me that my mother hadn't been right over the last few weeks. As she went on to say that they barely spoke anymore, I felt my stomach turn, wondering what had caused it. When I arrived for Easter, to prepare for whatever was waiting, I asked my father about her as we drove home from the train station.

"You know how she is. Stubborn. She still insists she's hearing things. She's like her father."

The house was oddly quiet as my father went back to his garden, my mother nowhere in sight.

"Mom?"

Hearing a loud "shhh," I walked toward the bathroom.

"I'm in here, Larry J. Be quiet or they'll hear us."

She was standing in the bathtub, staring out the window.

"The goddamned cats are at it again. They're coming for me."

As she turned to face me, I was horrified at the sight of her. Her face was drawn, and she was frighteningly thin. Looking in my direction, she was unable to meet my eyes.

"I'm here Mom." I said, trying to sound reassuring and calm.

She continued to talk, looking past me. I started to shake, terrified at what I was witnessing.

"Follow me," she whispered loudly in a gravelly voice. Then she tugged on my arm, and I joined her on the floor as we crawled into her bedroom. The house reeked of smoke, and as we approached her closet, I saw why. Cigarettes were everywhere. She picked up two that were half lit, from an ashtray piled high with butts, putting them both into her mouth. Her stained hands shook uncontrollably. I sat alone with her and tried to think of what to do while balancing the gravity of the situation.

"I'm going to have a look out the window again. Wait here," I told her.

She warned me to be careful, but she wasn't paying attention as she turned her gaze back to the ashtray. I stood distraught in the hallway, trying to gather myself. I went outside to where my father was humming in his garden.

"We need to get Mom to the hospital."

Barely looking up, he asked, "Why?"

I explained what I had just witnessed, and he stared blankly back, infuriating me.

"Dad, something is very wrong. We need to take her to the hospital."

I was stunned by his response. "Tomorrow. Don't ruin our Easter dinner."

Ignoring him, I got the doctor on the phone. He warned me how horrible it could be for all of us if the paramedics arrived and took her forcibly. I was afraid she'd never forgive me, but was determined to get her help, despite my father.

I found her tucked back into the closet, knees folded up to her chin, mouth full of lit cigarettes. I saw the singed ends of the sleeves and hems above her and was shocked she hadn't burned the house down.

"Mom, would you come with me if I promise to stay with you?"

She didn't look at me but answered, "Okay."

I helped her get onto the edge of the bed, but she was shaking so hard I had to take a firm grip, which caused her to wince.

"I want you to go with me to the doctor. I'm worried about your blood pressure. Can we do that?"

She looked at me warily and I added, "I spoke to your doctor. He thinks it's a good idea so you don't have another stroke."

She liked this doctor and nodded tentatively. With my arm wrapped tightly around her waist, I led her out into the bright light of the living room as she attempted to shield her eyes. Seeing my father, she looked at me and stopped.

"Not with him."

I grasped what she was saying. My only thought was to have her feel protected, so in a low, controlled voice, I said to him, "Take your own car."

He looked down and did as he was told.

I told the intake nurse I thought my mother was having a breakdown and filled her in on what I'd told my mother to get her there. The nurse was kind, and as she put her hand on mine, I felt relief for the first time that day.

She approached my mother, saying, "We're going to take you in and check your blood pressure. You're going to be fine."

I saw my mother was relenting, and I hoped some part of her believed she was now safe—from the voices, from hurting herself, and from the ignorance of my father. As they disappeared behind closed doors, my father tried to convince me she hadn't been that bad, that this was definitely her worst day. I couldn't stomach his words or excuses. I went to the car and sat alone inside, screaming through my sobs.

She was diagnosed as having psychotic depression with schizophrenic tendencies. My father refused to have her committed, choosing instead to rely on my mother's word that she'd remain as long as necessary.

This was, of course, short-lived. As she started medication and became less manic, the other patients convinced her that she didn't belong there. She had no memory of what had happened at home and how she'd gotten to the hospital. After less than a week, she signed herself out, believing she had been wronged.

When I asked my father what his plans were to prepare, he hesitated before asking me what I meant. He laughed at my suggestion of removing the guns and knives from the house, thinking it ludicrous. He insisted that checking in with the psychiatrist once a month for a medication evaluation was enough of a plan. He reminded me, repeatedly, "You know how stubborn she is. You can't make her do anything."

Short of moving back home and taking over their lives, I understood that any assistance I offered would be in vain. I did not understand the deep denial my father was living in, and knowing how my mother had deteriorated right in front of his eyes left me feeling bewildered. I realized that Eileen too had allowed denial to cloud her judgment, and I started wondering if I was the crazy one for thinking this was all wrong.

After a few more agonizing weeks, I broke the news to my father about Katherine. He was speechless at first, and then unleashed his accusations on me, saying I would regret messing up so badly. He asked how I could do this to them. He blamed me for putting him in the no-win situation of having to tell my mother, and questioned my compassion for their feelings. He stopped just short of saying I should patch things up for their sake.

Days passed before I heard from my mother, and when I did, her words stung.

"How could you do this to us? We loved her. Don't you ever bring another girl home again."

As I hung up, I laughed bitterly to myself. "I won't."

I was extremely emotional as the movers loaded the truck. Katherine held a placid calm and tried to make me laugh. She insisted this was our burden together, as she helped get me settled back in. I was dismayed by the condition of my old studio apartment. Not missing a beat, she cleaned, scrubbed, and directed the movers as they carried my belongings back up the three flights of steps. We said our goodbyes, and I listened at the door, hearing her shoes scuff against the tile floor. As she made her way down the second flight, out of sight, I heard her crying. My instinct was to run down and grab her, hold her, but I knew I couldn't. Instead, I quietly closed the door and got into bed, pulling the covers over my head.

The first few weeks were restless and exhausting. I had difficulty sleeping and found myself sitting up abruptly in the middle of the night as my heart raced and my body grew wet with sweat. I feared the nights when sleep evaded me, and I'd have no choice but to take to the streets, walking aggressively to exhaust myself. I moved briskly down avenues and side streets, jockeying between a sprint and a fast paced walk. I wondered how I was going to afford being back on my own, and even worse, what people thought of me with a broken engagement.

Katherine and I stayed in close touch, calling, sending notes, and even meeting for coffee, and she always appeared upbeat and comforting. I felt alone and conflicted about the freedom I felt from lying about who I was, and a looming sadness seemed to come from a place I couldn't reach.

I felt irritable at work but had to keep those feelings under control. I showed up earlier than my coworkers and often stayed late. I focused on busying myself constantly to prevent sadness from seeping in. As I faced an upcoming business trip to Oregon, I decided to take advantage of the time away and tacked on a week's vacation, to explore both the coastline and the potential for a career and geographic change. I was feeling claustrophobic. My apartment now seemed stiflingly small, and my nine-to-five job was conservative and mundane. I had to get out of the rut I was stuck in, and I believed the only solution was to change everything.

Anytime I called home to check in, my mother sounded sedated and succumbed to tears about Katherine. Her words irritated me, as she said how devastated they felt and how disappointed they were in me, but I forced myself to find words to placate them, often resorting to something along the lines of, "I know how hard this is for you, but please trust me that it was best for *both* of us." My assurances fell on deaf ears. They felt hurt and believed I had done it to them.

My trip to the west coast took me from rural Oregon to the coastline, the official start to my solo adventure. Before heading out of the mountains, I took one of the winding back roads out of town to explore the meadows and take in views of snow-capped mountains. Now that I was alone, I felt the weight of solitude and sadness plaguing me. I stopped along the edge of a pond and tried to soak in the chilly air, a stark contrast from the afternoon heat just a few miles back.

My heart was heavy, but I did not feel like crying. As I stared out ahead, it was as if I could see myself sitting there from above where my body sat, witnessing the despair from a distance. I was unnerved and became anxious, feeling my face flushed and my palms start to sweat. I stood abruptly, wanting to shake off these same feelings I had in New York, frustrated that I had not left them behind.

The roads heading out of the Cascade Mountain range were spectacular. I had done this drive once before with my colleagues, in awe of the far-reaching vistas and valleys below.

Now, in the car alone, I experienced gut-wrenching anxiety as I drove higher and higher. It was inexplicable that my body was now tense, and a queasy feeling resonated from deep within my groin. The lookout points were filled with tourists with cameras snapping the scenery, but for me, the idea of stopping along that incline meant I would undoubtedly fall to my death. Hands wet with sweat, I clenched the steering wheel as I stared at the road beyond the hood of my car.

A temporary reprieve occurred when I entered a town shadowed by towering pines that blocked the view. When I was able to think clearly, out of the fog of panic, I reminded myself how weak I had just been, and that I had exhibited the demeanor of a coward. I was able to shake it off.

I stopped all along the Oregon coast, as I made my way north toward Seattle. I loved the sea-swept towns, a far cry from the overpopulated beaches and boardwalks of the east coast. Here, the natural habitat was the main attraction, and I took walks through pine-scented forests, gathering pinecones. The haystack formations caught my attention, and as I gazed for hours, I lost myself in thoughts of what to do next.

I vacillated between being caught up in the beauty of my environment and an increasing sense of urgency.

Feeling restless, I returned from that trip and promptly resigned from my job. I felt a boost of confidence to have scored a new position with a competitor who offered me significantly more money. While I'd remain in New York, it would at least be something of a fresh start.

I received a letter from Penny expressing regret for how things had ended, and as I sat with her over coffee, I understood that my partner in crime had come back into my life at the perfect time. History was repeating itself, and as if no time had passed, we set out to reexamine and explore the city together. She was the friend I desperately needed.

Chapter Ten

Heading downtown to meet Penny, I took notice of a handsome man I passed on Mott Street. I noticed his cocky smirk first and returned the expression, and as our eyes locked, my body tingled. Caught up in the flirtation, I turned after passing him to see if he looked back. It was innocent enough, but I felt a disproportionate amount of disappointment that he did not look back at me.

Penny and I shuffled along, taking in the beautiful autumn day and remaining close to one another, arms around each other's waists. I noticed the handsome stranger was not far in front of us, and as he turned to walk into a gallery, Penny looked at me and simply raised her eyebrows. As we walked by, I saw the back of him as he faced photograph-lined walls. In an impulsive moment I never would have had without my mischievous counterpart on my arm, I reached into my pocket, pulling out a tiny notebook filled with creative ideas I hoped to tackle. I tore out a blank sheet and wrote my name and phone number on it.

"Go give this to that guy," I ordered confidently.

The look of surprise on Penny's face gave me a moment of doubt. "Are you sure?"

"Yes! Go do it," I blurted.

I stood nervously outside, watching her disappear through the door. After a moment, she rushed out, grabbed my hand, and said, "Let's get out of here."

We laughed as we raced down the street, me curious about what had transpired.

"He looked confused at first but then gave me a smile. I wonder if he'll call. I hope he's not a gay basher."

We laughed anxiously at the mere idea of this, but internally I feared the same thing as I thought back to high school. It was too late now.

On Monday, I threw myself into work, wanting to put the weekend out of my mind. I had stirrings of shame as I thought about what I had done. Had I just humiliated myself? I became critical of my appearance and doubted that his smirk was any sign of interest. Had he actually been mocking the skinny, longhaired guy who stared at him? I became convinced I had made a mistake, embarrassed I thought so much of myself in that moment.

The following weekend arrived quickly, and as I readied myself to get out and take in the day, the phone rang. Thinking it must be Penny, I answered casually. The voice on the other end was not a woman's.

"Yeah, hi. You gave me your number last weekend on the street."

We stammered along in an awkward conversation for a few minutes, until he managed to eke out a suggestion for a lunch date. He told me his name was David. I felt the same stirring I had upon seeing him for the first time.

With the exception of James, I was still new to the concept of going on a date with a man. I was much more accustomed to detached encounters that left no trace of real connection, other than physical. I was apprehensive, but couldn't ignore how seeing him and hearing his voice made me feel. We agreed to meet at a spot near my office.

As I got ready that morning, I concerned myself with what to wear. I pulled out a pair of tight brown wool slacks that left nothing to the imagination, and a fitted turtleneck sweater.

It was an exceptionally beautiful day, and as I walked in, I smiled bashfully. David was about my height, with a solid body and pronounced features. I took my seat across from him, and my stomach churned in excitement as he told me about his work, his Brooklyn upbringing, and living in Manhattan. I listened intently to everything he had to say. My hands shook with nerves, which he clearly noticed as he repeatedly looked down, and my attempts to steady them on the table failed. I limited the details about my upbringing and focused more on the present day and my relatively new job. As we finished lunch, he offered to walk me back to my office. I caught his eyes scanning my body and wondered what he was thinking. I took it as a good sign that lunch lasted well over an hour and he had not rushed out afterward. We hugged as we said goodbye. Once alone, in my office, I tried to digest how excited I felt.

David had a cocky, laissez-faire attitude about him, which I found both sexy and infuriating. He casually mentioned he'd call to make a plan for the following weekend, and as the days passed and I didn't hear from him, I was heartsick. I replayed our lunch over and over in my mind, wondering where I had gone wrong. I picked apart my choice of clothing, convinced he found me too skinny.

As Saturday approached, I gathered up the courage to call him, something I swore I wouldn't do for fear of being rejected. He sounded pleasantly surprised to hear from me, as if he had forgotten he said he'd call. I was tentative but determined after hearing the tone of his voice. We would meet again for our second date the following evening. I hung up the phone feeling triumphant.

I spent most of the day leading up to our date thinking about what to bring him. I stumbled into an old-fashioned candy store and selected two marzipan ladybugs. They were charming, cheery, and out of the ordinary—not your average bottle of wine or flowers. I didn't want to be average, and wanted desperately to impress him. His apartment was at Eighteenth and Park Avenue, and as he buzzed me in, my nerves skyrocketed. I took the elevator up to the top floor and was intrigued by the loft architecture, a stark contrast from the stained and crumbling tile floors of the tenement I inhabited. As he greeted me, I extended my hand. He looked at it and laughed, taking me into his arms. I presented my gift, and he revealed tenderness as he looked inside, thanking me with a subtle grin.

Our childhoods could not have been more different. David grew up in Brooklyn in a traditional Syrian Jewish home, with three older siblings. He went to NYU and worked as a foreign currency trader. He was not out to his family, and like me, he had been with women and had come close to marriage. We compared notes about dating and heterosexual sex and our discomfort fitting into the gay community. Not only did he listen, but he also understood and was able to relate to my struggles and doubts.

As we spent more time together, I had no reservation admitting to myself that I had fallen in love. I questioned the fast pace of my feelings, but they matched my energy and the constant buzz I felt pulsing through my bloodstream. It was an old feeling, an anxious longing I had always carried with me. I ignored any voices of doubt and allowed myself to succumb to my attraction and admiration for him.

David accepted my distaste for anal sex. We were enamored with each other's bodies and discovered over time what was most pleasurable. I could not believe my good fortune at having found a man who did not pressure me into that kind of sex, something I had believed was a prerequisite to being gay. I added this to the long list of reasons we were destined for one another. David, eleven years older, had the confidence I lacked, and as he shared it willingly, I wanted to learn from his example.

Within a few months of meeting, I was ready to move in with him. I nagged him incessantly, revealing the demanding and stubborn streak I had inherited from my mother. I couldn't accept his hesitation. Why didn't he want to jump as quickly and as completely as I had? I was placing demands on this man, the same way my mother had demanded so much of my father. I was his first significant male relationship, and I was asking for something that was not only new to him but also went beyond what he was yet comfortable with. He still had his family and friends to face about his sexuality, let alone explain a live-in boyfriend.

Not only was I swept away by David's way of life, I also saw it as an opportunity to distance myself further from where I had come from. When we were together, I felt important and noticed, and I wanted to feel that way all the time. Living together was sure to solve it. I couldn't get enough of feeling wanted and appreciated. He spent money freely and seemingly without worry; he was cultured and had a carefree approach to life that was foreign to a guy who was often consumed by worry. I craved a way of life that would elevate my self-worth, and I was certain that by living together, I could provide David with the nurturing and attention I knew he craved. In return, I'd feel secure. I hated that I feared the vulnerability of living alone. I saw the greater potential of what we could create together. I couldn't stop to consider my feelings of urgency; I just needed to trust them.

As we prepared for a trip to Paris and the south of France to visit one of his closest friends, he asked me to do him a favor.

"Lar, while we're away, would you please not bring up living together? I need more time to think about it, and I'd love to just enjoy ourselves on this trip."

Feeling embarrassed that I had clearly become a nuisance, I agreed. "I promise."

We arrived and inhaled everything about the City of Lights. I regaled him with tales of my trip there with Katherine, and quietly recognized the deep satisfaction I felt being there with him. It was a city in which our love for each other intensified, made even more compact by our love of food, wine, and art. We strolled aimlessly through gardens and parks and caught each other's gaze as our shoulders touched and hands grazed each other's thighs. It was magical, and I felt caught up in the deep joy I was experiencing, feeling complete with this man at my side. On our final day, he took me to the Picasso Museum. Like a child, I could no longer contain my frustration. The preceding days had me even more convinced that we were meant for each other, and once outside in the garden, I blurted out, "I just don't understand why you haven't asked me yet!"

The look on his face was crushing. I had broken my word. He glared at me and said nothing. I feared I had just sabotaged our future.

We recovered from the soured energy within a few days and got through the rest of the vacation. I tried to remain pleasant and undemanding. His friend who lived in the south of France clearly did not like me. It felt like my punishment for bad behavior, as she refused to engage me in their conversations and barely disguised her lack of interest in me. I kept my mouth shut and remained as close to David as he would allow.

Once we got back and resumed city living, he tearfully asked if I'd live with him. As I heard his words, I felt elated and the tiniest bit nervous at the same time. I ignored the small piece of self-doubt that crept up as I worried about what others would think, and if I was really ready for this commitment. I was getting what I had nagged and begged for, validation and security. I took a few months to settle on a new tenant to sublet my studio, wanting to hold onto it as an insurance policy should things not work out. David poked fun at me because now I was dragging my feet.

Eileen immediately accepted David. We talked about how best to tell my parents. As far as I was concerned, nothing was up for discussion in terms of the relationship. I did not want to acknowledge the anger that lingered from being outed and called a faggot by my mother, and I felt a resolve to approach them with a take-it-or-leave-it attitude. Eileen, sensing it might not go so well, offered to speak to my father first, to sort out what was best in terms of my mother.

When I spoke to my father on the phone, his voice stirred my anger. My jaw clenched as I explained if they treated me like they had before, they would never see me again. I wasn't sure I meant it, but in that moment, I mustered all my courage.

Sounding crushed, he quietly said, "I'll speak to your mother."

After a few agonizing days, I was both relieved and defensive when she called. She was surprisingly upbeat, and I thought her medication was clearly working, hoping this new mom was permanent. She remained kindhearted as she recounted what my sister and father had told her. She asked me what David did, and I said he worked on Wall Street. She cheered, "Way to go," exhibiting a difference in her personality that was astonishing. I spoke of his kindness and how happy I felt, and that culturally we were different but it made things that much richer. We chatted for a few more minutes until her voice went serious.

"Larry J., we would really like to meet him, but you have to do something for me."

I braced myself for what was to come.

"Please don't tell your father he's Jewish."

I bit my lip to avoid laughing. The magnitude of the conversation was lost on her, as she shifted the focus to their shared prejudice that ironically had nothing to do with my sexuality.

"Okay, Mom. Whatever you want."

My parents embraced the idea of David immediately. All the routines established with Katherine were now enacted with him: holiday gifts, gratitude for bringing their son home, and the constant need for us to visit more frequently. But the ease in which everyone settled into David's arrival into my life was unnerving. It felt too good to be true, as if there were an ulterior motive to their radical change of heart and acceptance. Once again, I was waiting for the inevitable tide to change, feeling unprepared for what was to come.

As David faced the daunting task of coming out to his siblings and parents, I wondered what would unfold. Would they accept him? Me? Us? He grew up in a family where such things were not generally discussed. With rare exception, homosexuality was not accepted, and his father's use of offensive language gave David enough of a reason to feel the hesitation to be honest. Armed with one of his sisters, he went to New Jersey, where they now lived, and broke the news over lunch. After they absorbed what he told them, he went on to say there was someone in his life he would like them to meet. The day had gone far better than he had anticipated. We were both relieved.

When the day arrived for me to meet his parents, I worried what they would think of this young, skinny, Lutheran boy from Pennsylvania.

I was not only entering their lives, but an entire world of insular Syrian Jews. It was a culture completely foreign to me. We were invited for lunch, and as we walked into their apartment, I was immediately taken in by their hospitality. Camille, his elegant mother set an incredible table as his father took his place at the head of it. I was amazed at the feast put out before us, and as my eyes grew with astonishment, David gave me a smile that put me at ease.

He whispered in my direction, "This is how we do it. You'll never go hungry." There he was, the mystery man from Mott Street sitting with me over an elaborate meal in his parents' home. In that moment I felt worthy and special, and I promised to find ways to make him feel the same way.

As I was swept up in my new relationship, my career caught the same tide of change. I got a call from the company I had resigned from months earlier, offering a position I could not refuse. They knew I had been unhappy and went out of their way to create a generous proposal.

Within a few months, I was able to pay off my student loans and easily contribute my share to our household. Along with my income, my ego grew, and just as I had been impatient and impulsive with David, I now applied this to every area of my life, indulging in more and better on a regular basis. I had found a new way of dissipating the undeniable pang of anxiety that resided in me. Eating, drinking, traveling, spending—all became solutions to any unpleasant sensations that threatened to rise to the surface. If I remained vigilant, I could keep them under control.

David and I submerged ourselves in the splendors of two lucrative careers. We travelled more extensively and loved how seamlessly we existed with one another. In the city, we indulged in lunches and dinners that made me swoon. We felt ignited by tasting menus and reveled in the hype of new, trendy restaurants. I feared embarrassing David with my Levittown ways, and made great efforts to become the person I "should" be. I watched and listened like an attentive student as I learned how to properly order my martinis. "Vodka, up, extra cold, extra dry, three olives, please," fell off my tongue as effortlessly as "Good morning." We enjoyed drinks before dinner, and at least two bottles of wine perfectly paired with our meals. Any notion that I was drinking too much was dismissed, as we remained lost in the ceremony of it. I was so enamored with him that I rarely got through a meal without my eyes filling with tears. I could not believe how my life had turned around, how all those years of doubt and fear paved the way to what I was now experiencing. I was transitioning into a life that felt worlds away from all that.

David owned his apartment, and when I met him, he had just completed a long and beautifully designed renovation. Forever restless, I struggled with the open living plan and craved a space of my own. I did not want to admit the echoing sounds across the hard floors and high ceilings made me jittery and the smells emanating from the kitchen brought up unpleasant memories of my tumultuous upbringing.

I was embarrassed that I couldn't separate then from now, and could not accept how anxious I felt all the time.

After weekends exploring away from the city, we settled on the idea of a country house in the Hudson Valley. In just a few short weeks, we agreed on a late Victorian farmhouse that was situated on a hill across from a river. We shuttled ourselves back and forth on the two-hour drive, rarely missing a weekend.

The house gave me an outlet for the hyper-drive I operated in. I obsessed over the gardens and planted bulbs by the hundreds. The interior received a cosmetic overhaul, and I jammed the rooms with antiques and flea market finds I scoured for obsessively. For many people, weekends were a time to relax, but I became unstoppable in my need to constantly alter and improve. I loved it all. I worked to the point of exhaustion, and by the time Sunday evening rolled around, I was irritable and depressed, not wanting to go back to the city.

David, too, had fallen in love with upstate New York. He had been unhappy in his career, and now feeling more settled in domesticity, started to outline his plans to resign. We were approaching a dreaded trip with my family, but David used it as his turning point. Upon our return, he would terminate his Wall Street employment and look toward new opportunities as he faced turning forty. We looked at things as a couple and together could tackle anything that lay ahead of us.

The idea of a family vacation nauseated me. The thought of those trips as a kid and how my mother inevitably acted out made me shudder. My niece was now five, and Eileen and her husband wanted to take her to Disney World, asking my parents and David and me to join them. David, always willing to please me, didn't quite appreciate how much I needed him at my side. I did not feel that I could bear it alone, knowing my father would seize this as an opportunity for family time, to do everything together. As we checked into the hotel, the desk clerk informed me that my family had already arrived. I turned to David with a forced grin and said, "Here we go."

We got to our room, hoping to sneak in some time alone before the family reunion. Within minutes, we heard knocking at the door. Finding no one there, the knock continued. As David realized the knock was from the door adjoining the room next door, he opened it to find my father standing on the other side. My chest tightened as he told us how lucky he was to secure adjoining rooms. When I asked where Eileen was, he explained they were on another floor, in what was meant to be our room. He wanted father-son time, and my mother did not want to be in close proximity to my niece. My mother yelled from their bed, saying she was lying down because of her arthritis, sending me the reminder in case I'd forgotten. We went in to greet her as she started to cry, telling us she was in so much pain she wasn't sure how she was going to get through the week. Privately, I wondered the same thing about me.

The trip was a nightmare from then on. My father insisted we leave the doors open, growing frustrated any time we tried to have some privacy.

"Leave it open. It feels more like home."

I felt distraught over the intrusion, and angry that within the first twenty-four hours, I was made to feel guilty if I got up to close the door. I kept those feelings to myself, too embarrassed to admit them out loud. What would David think? He didn't understand what my father was like, I told myself. He wouldn't understand that we had to make him feel loved and accepted after a life of being repeatedly rejected by his wife.

As we set to out to explore the theme parks, my mother refused a wheelchair, but became irate and emotional as her knees ached, and she walked slowly behind us. Causing a scene, she sat on the wall of a fountain sobbing until one of us went to comfort her. After our endless pleading, she finally submitted to assistance. We took turns pushing the wheelchair as she cried, saying this was her fate, to be wheelchair-bound for the rest of her life. We appeased her with stuffed animals, chocolate, a new sweatshirt—anything to not have her ruin a vacation that was intended for a five-year-old, who we discovered was terrified by Disney characters. The vacation unfolded hourly with new twists and adventures, culminating on September 11, 2001.

David had taken my mother to a spa, treating her to a massage. As the horrors of the morning burst into reality, I hurried to find him, because I'd heard evacuation of all the parks had been ordered. As we watched the spa television monitor in horror, we tried to absorb the incomprehensible reality of what was happening back in New York.

My mother was told of the attacks by her massage therapist, but asked that she continue with her massage anyway. We waited impatiently for her to come out, and when we told her we had to get back to the hotel, she became indignant, complaining she had not yet had her special spa lunch. In a rare moment, David snapped and made it clear that we were not going anywhere but back to the room. She remained silent, pouting like a child in her wheelchair, as David faced gut-wrenching phone calls back home to his coworkers.

He and I wasted no time in securing a rental car and made the decision to drive back to New York the following day. My father wanted us all to drive together, an idea that made my stomach turn, but my mother insisted her vacation not be ruined any further, and that the long drive back was too much for her. For once, I enthusiastically agreed with her, and internally thanked her for being self-centered in that particular moment.

David's industry rallied as best it could, but he felt an obligation to stay until things stabilized. He made no mention of his plans to resign, and we took the apartment, which we had decided to sell, off of the market as we waited with the rest of the world to see what would happen next.

As we settled into the promises of a new year, things started to unfold from the tight ball they had been contained in. David regained his footing and gave his company six weeks' notice. We accepted an offer on the apartment and rented a place in a high-rise along the West Side Highway, allowing us to get out of the city and upstate that much faster. David planned to take a year off before deciding on his next move, but that was short-lived when he became restless after a few months.

We knew we wanted to move to the Hudson Valley, and he felt ready to take that leap. He took an expedited real estate course and got his license over the summer, moving into the upstate house. The distance from each other was challenging, but he assured me it would all work out in the long run and the inconvenience was only temporary.

We were at the halfway point in figuring out how to redefine our lives. He learned the real estate market in the towns that surrounded us, and I continued to work in the city. With some financial security in place, I focused my attention on making my dream of an antique and home furnishings store a reality. David was our spy, keeping an eye out for any opportunities that might present themselves. I did not enjoy being in the city without him. As my anxiety reached new levels, I worked hard at keeping it hidden. I drank heavily, losing myself to evenings of false camaraderie at bars up and down Ninth Avenue. I numbed my pang of envy as his excitement about his new career became more evident.

In a particularly tense moment when my frustration reared its head, David suggested I meet with the therapist who helped with his own career transition. Reluctantly I agreed. I knew I only had to reveal what I deemed important and thought it would expedite our plans to regroup. I saw it as an express lane to getting what I needed to complete our picture. I did not do slow or steady. Quick fixes were the only way I knew to stay afloat.

David found the building that would become the home of our future business. It would need significant work, but the price was fair, and we would be able to renovate it exactly how we envisioned. In the spring, we closed on the purchase of our new endeavor. That same afternoon, I drove into the city and resigned. The therapist and I had planned for this day, and everything had gone smoothly. While my employers were disappointed, I was willing to stay on for as long as necessary for them to hire my replacement. I was grateful to be leaving a career that had earned me a robust income with my reputation and relationships intact. It was the best possible springboard to launch me into the unknown territory of life outside of New York City. I hadn't burned any bridges, something new to me as far as relationships were concerned.

I decided to continue speaking with the therapist through phone sessions from the house. I believed he would be helpful in planning out how best to tackle all that was in front of me. I shared more than I had originally planned, and often felt sad and vulnerable when our discussions leaned toward my emotions.

The timing of my life shift conspired against me, landing in the middle of summer. I struggled to understand why, in the middle of watching my dreams form into reality, I was feeling an overwhelming sense of despair. I moved through the days tentatively, not wanting to let this dark side emerge.

I worked diligently to pull together all the details for the new business. I came up with systems that would keep me organized and focused, and sourced unique and hard-to-come-by inventory. I insisted on the best of everything. In terms of what I felt I needed to fulfill my vision, there was no compromise. If David expressed any concern about a budget or business plan, I bulldozed over him, giving him no option but to show his support or face the consequences of my increasingly irrational behavior.

I convinced myself that this was my opportunity to prove I could be something. The business became interwoven with my identity, and I set out to show I was no longer that Levittown boy.

At home, away from the chaos of the building's renovation, I'd try to embrace the quiet. I felt increasingly nervous being alone and hated the rare occasions David went into the city or to Boston to visit his best friend. I was convinced that while alone, we would be robbed or someone would come for me during the night. I was too terrified to sleep in our upstairs bedroom and felt I had an advantage if I stayed in our small den on the first floor with faster access to getting out.

I tried to drink myself into a stupor, washing down handfuls of valerian and melatonin tablets, but my adrenaline raced so high, that only made me jumpy. I slept clutching my car keys in a plan to make a quick getaway. I woke to any small sound, and my fractured sleep left me feeling vulnerable and emotional the next day. I would not admit such a weakness to David, in fear that he would see me as less than capable to open my own business, let alone be his partner.

On a therapy phone session, I confessed cryptically to feeling vulnerable. I spoke of my self-doubt and allowed some of my fears and insecurities to emerge. I felt my chest tighten as I listened for what the therapist might say next. I answered his limited questions about my upbringing abruptly and with as little detail as possible. As he suggested that some of what I was saying sounded like it was based in shame, possibly from childhood, I wanted the session to be over. I stood and paced around the room as he continued his thoughts about anxiety. When he said feelings of shame could have long-term effects, I started to cry, letting my pent up tears erupt. He concluded that we should speak again the following week, and after agreeing, I ended the call and broke down sobbing. I did not understand what was happening, but I knew enough to feel embarrassed.

When David came in to find out if I was okay, I pulled myself together, reassuring both of us that I was fine. I left the therapist a message terminating our relationship, giving the excuse that I was now too busy to continue therapy. I thanked him profusely and set out to keep my mind and body as busy as I possibly could. I feared the sadness that had overtaken me, understanding that if I allowed it any more space, it might consume me. I couldn't let that happen.

I put my entire focus and all my efforts into pushing to get the store opened for the following spring season.

Our big reveal in a small town was no small task. We ordered hand-letter-pressed invitations, had a preview dinner party for our closest friends and family, and planned an all-day open house. My father beamed with pride, introducing himself as LJ's father. He was charming and engaging, and spoke of how proud he was that I had turned a childhood passion into something real. I avoided listening to these conversations, having endured his doubt and criticisms. Now, as he saw the magnitude of what I was doing, he acted as if he wanted to own it as his achievement. Seeing my mother sitting alone, half empty glass of champagne in hand, I took a seat on the bench, putting my arm around her. As I pulled her close, she started to cry. I told her I was glad she was there, but she pulled away from me.

"I hate this store."

Caught off guard, I asked, "Why would you say that?"

"It's going to take you away from me. I'll never see you now. I hate it."

The anger was evident on her face—the face I knew better than my own.

Chapter Eleven

The terror that seized me in the car in Oregon revisited me in the Hudson Valley whenever I drove at high elevations. With David along, I tried to laugh off my sweaty palms and rapid heartbeat as we crossed the Hudson River, driving across the bridge from Kingston to Rhinebeck. Going it alone was another story. When I tried to drive across the George Washington Bridge into Manhattan, the formerly benign crossing turned into a living nightmare as the traffic came to a halt, and I found myself sitting with an unobstructed view of the water below. Gazing up at the soaring architecture, I became certain it would collapse. My chest pounded and I was drenched with sweat as I sat there motionless, trying to figure out what to do.

This had become my new normal whenever I crossed a bridge or drove at the slightest elevation. My shallow breathing was the only thing I could focus on as I attempted to watch the road in front of me for any signs that cars were moving. Once I'd arrived at my destination, I'd berate myself: *What a foolish thing to have happen.* I decided the only way to not feel that again was to avoid those routes.

Before I hired help for my blossoming business, David covered if I felt the pull of obligation to visit my parents. I tried to prove my mother's doubts wrong during each of my visits. She hit a nerve whenever she commented on my drinking, and I still carried some belief she saw me as a faggot, despite her seeming acceptance of David. I couldn't shake her words from so many years earlier. I did not want her to feel justified in her claims that my business was going to take me away from her, but the truth was it was an all-consuming endeavor that did prohibit me from giving her the kind of attention she demanded.

To battle the conflicted emotions I had about not seeing her more often, I sent her surprises and gifts from my shop. So much of what I sold was more sophisticated than she was used to, and I took pride in introducing her to new things. If I sent something for my father, his standard response was, "Save your money. It's you I want, not some overpriced thing from your store."

When I visited, I'd treat them to expensive dinners. I felt I had to go out of my way to find methods of placating them. I believed it would alleviate the underlying feeling that I was a disappointment. Once I went so far as to send them to Las Vegas for their anniversary. To add to the surprise, David and I flew across the country to join them for a few days. They cried as they saw us coming toward them, and we lavished them with tickets to shows, meals, and money for gambling. In my effort to control the dynamics, David and I stayed at a different hotel altogether. There would be no adjoining rooms this time.

When I made the first drive from upstate New York to Levittown after my panic attacks returned, I did not anticipate anything going wrong. There would be limited highways and extensive back roads, and I felt confident I could navigate the narrow crossing of the Delaware River if I did it quickly. I kept my mind focused on the music in the car, and tried not to think about the visit ahead.

The lanes shifted as I entered New Jersey en route to Pennsylvania, and I felt the telltale sensation deep in my groin. As I sensed the elevation increase, my hands trembled. The view in front of me was clear. The highway was elevated in spots and climbed up along craggy rocks of a steep hillside. I understood I was in trouble as my entire body fell into what was now a regular painful experience. I slowed in the left lane as cars honked and whizzed by. I felt that if I crept along steadily, I might make it to the other side. My gaze remained just beyond the end of the hood as I shook, wet from perspiration. That route had multiple inclines and long vistas from elevated points, mocking me as I tried to maintain my composure. No sooner did I arrive at my parents' house before the fear of reversing my path took over. I decided to wait until nightfall, which would be a temporary solution, as the darkness would camouflage whatever I faced beyond the windshield.

I sensed trouble brewing again. My mother seemed more emotional, and the scores of boxes that arrived daily from QVC didn't seem to be appeasing her. My father complained bitterly about my mother's constant spending, as the credit card bills skyrocketed. When I suggested that perhaps he should take the cards away from her, he sharply criticized me.

"You don't understand. It's the only thing that is making her feel better. I'm telling you because I have no one to talk to, not because I want your opinion."

He insisted he would not refuse her a few small gifts, and reminisced about the times he bought me souvenirs and piled Christmas presents high under the tree.

"And don't forget how much I helped you in college. Remember that?"

My mind clouded as I tried to sort out the checks and balances of our lives together, and I was left confused, wondering if I was doing enough. I felt sick as I thought of the meals, trips, and gifts. Perhaps providing these things was viewed as a requisite of their only son: to do for them what he felt they had done for me.

After my visit, I received a call from Eileen that added an additional layer of worry.

"I think Dad is having financial problems. He's late on his mortgage by a few months."

I heard my sister's words and felt the punch in my stomach.

"He's afraid to ask you for help, but I don't think he has a choice."

I understood she was a part of this equation, and he knew she was making the call. We were trained to avoid confrontation at any costs, and here was my father doing just that. Eileen had her own string of financial woes and was straddled with bills as she attempted to stay afloat. It was out of the question that she was in a position to do anything; after all, she had a child, and her daughter was her priority. I was the successful brother and son who didn't have children. They turned to me knowing I wouldn't be able to say no.

Together, David and I made a trip out to talk to them and find out how bad things were. We were resigned to helping them get out of their bind. As we pulled into the driveway, I said to him, "I'm dreading this."

He squeezed my hand and reassured me it would all work out.

Neatly stacked piles of bills and papers covered the dining room table. My mother greeted us, and as she started to cry, she excused herself, retreating to the bedroom and shutting the door behind her.

"Mom should be a part of this discussion," I said to my father.

"She doesn't want to be here. She's nervous about what you guys are going to say. Let's leave her alone," he replied defensively.

I was annoyed that she was being protected from accountability but chose not to start a disagreement during what was already proving to be a challenging talk. The scenario my father went on to lay out in front of us over the next hour was disturbing. Their credit cards bills were in the tens of thousands of dollars, and they had taken out a second mortgage. He was underwater and blamed his generosity for getting him into that predicament. He told David about how he had spoiled all of us, and just couldn't say no. He told us of his own childhood with an absent father and a depressed mother, and he was determined to give us all a better experience than he had had.

Looking up, he let out a big sigh and said, "But now, well, things have caught up with me. It's the price you pay for being a loving and generous father and husband."

The QVC charges gave an honest portrayal of what was happening during the day. My mother seemed to believe that the hosts of the show were her friends and would not steer her wrong. The velour outfits and cubic zirconia jewelry would do just as they told her and make her feel special and noticed. She was in desperate need of something to soothe her aching joints, so she turned to shopping. Her level of self-absorption was apparent on her fingers, each one adorned with at least one ring. Around her neck there were layers of chains that matched what studded her ears. When I commented on the repetitive charges, my father told me we would have to speak to her together and come up with a plan to get her to decrease her spending. I saw that this whole intervention was already more complex than David and I had bargained for.

David was incredibly patient with my parents. While he did not like the noticeable impact they had on my well-being, he was sympathetic. We agreed to purchase their house, allowing them to remain there with an affordable rent, enough to cover the mortgage we would have to take out. The deal came with conditions. My father would have to pay off all the credit cards and mortgages and not incur any additional debt. David would handle the logistics and arrange for appraisals and lawyers. My father thanked us and made a joke about having us as landlords, which made me cringe. I hated that he was already making light of the situation but tried to shake it off, thinking it might be his embarrassment over having to ask us for help.

My father excused himself to get my mother and share the "good news" with her. I felt like the parent to my parents. I was embarrassed that my father showed no signs of regret or remorse. He acted as if he had been given a free pass. His exuberance at accepting our bailout made me wonder if David would change his mind once we were alone. But he remained supportive and put my concerns to rest, reassuring me that we would do the same thing for his family if they needed it.

His generosity overwhelmed me.

On the day of the closing, I drove out alone to sign the contracts. The journey was worse than it had been previously. I was angry with David for not being with me, even though I had insisted I could handle things on my own. I vacillated between wanting David there and not wanting to burden him any further. My father beamed as I walked into the lawyer's office, and my mother looked confused and relieved at the same time. I was edgy and uncomfortable, feeling nauseated from my harrowing drive. I smiled and greeted my parents warmly, not wanting to let on that anything was wrong.

After the deal was finalized, my mother hugged me, asking me if I had time to have lunch before heading back. I could feel a migraine coming on quickly, and apologized, reassuring her I'd be back again soon. My father finished up his smarmy conversation with the lawyer and walked me down the hallway toward the parking lot. He pulled me aside and gave me a firm hug, pulling me in close to his body. I felt myself go rigid as he whispered in my ear, "Thank you, Son. You always knew how to make your old man feel better."

I couldn't breathe. Walking out to my car, my nausea intensified. I had to throw up, but there was no time to go back inside, and I couldn't face them again.

I sat in my car intermittently vomiting and dry heaving, as tears fell down my face. I couldn't shed his soft voice whispering in my ear and his breath on my neck. The fear and repulsion I felt stirred deep within, and I wanted it to come out. I kept trying to throw up, purge whatever it was from my mind and my body, but my tears kept coming, and I felt lost and alone. I could not make sense of this sickness that swirled in me. I thought of driving off, and forgetting all this had happened. Everything in this moment was a bad dream, and I wanted out.

I struggled to regain my footing after buying the house. I had made an enormous mistake. Too embarrassed to admit that to David, I instead became angry and short-tempered. I wanted to put the whole thing out of my mind, but I couldn't. Distracted, I attempted to throw myself into big projects, only to find I was incapable of focusing on any one thing for too long. My solace had always been to delve into merchandising and designing, but now I left things half finished, with the messes I created staring back at me spitefully.

I had worked so hard to remove myself from feeling the stain of Levittown and now, more than ever, it was a part of me.

You own that hell hole. You're an idiot.

In rare moments, I could rationalize that it was a real estate investment—just as David had referred to it—but in reality that house was now a part of my life, and it repulsed me. My father didn't help. He made comments about his landlords being tough on him and reminded me of how fortunate we were to have him living there, taking such good care of the house that was sure to earn us a healthy return. I was startled when he said that down the road, once it was time to sell, he felt at ease knowing David and I would split the profits with Eileen. When I pressed him on how he saw it that way, he became angry, reminding me it was now my responsibility to make sure my family was cared for.

I thought my erratic behavior was justified. I was running my own business, and David was running his. I needed help but did not know how to ask for it without demands and ultimatums. I grew increasingly anxious and fought it any way I could.

I went to the gym obsessively, worked nonstop, and at the end of the day, couldn't wait for a martini to take away the frustrations or honor the victories. I had earned those drinks, and indulged in them frequently and with conviction. While I thought I was concealing the majority of my nervous state, David had noticed. Changing the subject quickly during a difficult confrontation one evening, I expected him to say something to anger me further, perhaps suggest I was being unreasonable.

Instead, he looked me in the eye and said, "I think you need to see someone. Something isn't right."

I felt found out. I worried that he saw me for what I believed I was, an anxious mess of a man who was unhinged. But as our eyes met, I knew I trusted David. I refused to let him in on the whole truth—what had happened after the sale of the house and the anxiety that kept me up at night. I would lie awake for hours thinking about what to do next, how to be better, stronger, faster. My chest felt like it had hundreds of pounds of weight strapped to it, and I often found it hard to breathe.

Instinctively I felt relieved that he had made this suggestion. In my frenetic thoughts, I questioned if I was going down the same mental illness path as my mother.

The therapist I was referred to had an extensive form to fill out, which I half-heartedly tackled. I did not want to be bothered with such things. I wanted a quick solution to better handle my parents, and tackle the day-to-day things that life was throwing my way. At first I kept details to a minimum, making it clear I had an important job, I had my shit together, and I had been in therapy before and was skeptical. She listened, nodded, and absorbed what I was saying. I did not want to talk about what happened to me when I drove over bridges or elevations, or the episode of throwing up after buying my parents' house, and I most certainly did not want to discuss my drinking.

To combat the shame I felt, I created a life that was in stark contrast to how I grew up. The store I owned and operated catered to the type of people I respected: successful, wealthy, and cultured. The things I sold were the best of the best—beautiful table linen, apothecary, and furniture—and I demanded the same for myself. Anything less would be unacceptable and would show that I was not living up to the required image. My personal identity became so intertwined with my business that it became impossible for me to separate them. If the store looked dirty or disorganized, then I, too, was dirty and disorganized. When something was out of place in my meticulous alignment of objects, I believed it was a direct reflection of my talent and ability. Completing a window display or vignette left me feeling accomplished, but if I failed to finish I convinced myself that I was a failure. I cleaned and rearranged obsessively, always needing to keep things looking inspired and inviting.

I had no patience waiting for someone to help, and when I did ask David and he failed to materialize immediately, the derision I projected filled the room with tension. I much preferred to haul armoires and fixtures across the shop on my own, ignoring the bruises and increasingly tight muscles in my back, neck, and shoulders. I knew that any pain that I experienced was worth the gratification I felt from knowing I could accomplish my vision for the interior of the shop without needing anyone's help. I would fight weakness to the end. The high prices on things became a way of placing value on me as a person, and I came to believe that a price tag should not be an obstacle to having fine things. As I elevated my business, I would feel temporarily elevated. I charmed customers and scored bigger and more exclusive projects with my feigned sophistication and confidence. My interior design roster soared as a result, and as my hourly rate rose, so did my ego. There was no half way. It was all or nothing. I demanded it in all areas of my life. More was better, and no one could convince me otherwise.

My parents' visits were difficult. They would come on weekends, my busiest time, and take their places in the store. My father insisted on standing behind the counter, surveying the activity. My mother found her place on a sofa or chair and would comment, whispering a little too loudly about a handbag, outfit, or hairstyle of the browsing customers. If I tried to get them to sit in the back room, my mother gave me her look of scorn. My father was adamant that he stay put, claiming his position as the proprietor's father. When I objected to his intrusive stance, he ignored me, rationalizing that he didn't get to spend enough time with me, and that this store was something he was not only proud of, but also felt included in.

One of the few benefits of our decision to move to the apartment above the store was that we were short on accommodations. Whenever my family made a trip to see us, I paid for them to stay in a local bed and breakfast, making sure they felt welcome by giving them gifts when they arrived and handling any expenses they incurred. It was a given that they were not in a position to contribute financially. As my father liked to remind me, "I wouldn't want to be short on the rent this month. I've got a tough landlord. I might get evicted!"

I watched how much I drank in front of my mother. I did not want to give her any cause to further comment. I also hoped that if I drank less, she would follow my lead. The evenings would end with her tearful as she thanked me for taking care of her and making her feel special. My father's hugs were long and firm, as he nuzzled his face into my neck and told me how much he loved me. By the time Sunday afternoon rolled around, I was eager to see their car pulling away from the building. As soon as the car was out of sight, I'd slip into a drunken stupor, drinking martinis as I tried to wash away another weekend that left me feeling filthy.

The Hudson Valley is a bucolic place to live with its farms, Catskill Mountains views, and winding country roads. I had done the scenic drive over Minnewaska numerous times and thought nothing of it, as I headed over the mountain to get from one town to the other. As I rounded the hairpin turn and felt the car start to climb, the unmistakable sensation in my gut started to make itself known. I felt panicked, recognizing what was happening. *Why here? Why now?* As my car emerged for the vast scenic views of what lie ahead and below, my body tensed and tingled as sweat oozed from my pores. I inched to my left, farther away from the sharp drop on my right. Before I realized what I was doing, I had slowed the car so much that it was barely moving as I maneuvered in the opposite lane. Cars swerved to miss colliding with me head on. I crept along and assumed my gaze just beyond the hood as if in a trance.

Reentering tree-covered terrain, I resumed my place in the correct lane and wiped my face with my sleeve and dried my hands on the leg of my pants. I told myself this was not normal. I felt defective and argued that I should be stronger and rational when I was behind the wheel. I was disgusted with myself. Had someone recognized my car? What if it were David or a client coming toward me as I drove in the wrong lane? I felt humiliated and feared being discovered.

I saw the therapist weekly. Slowly, I spoke more of my parents and how they made me feel during their visits. She spoke of boundaries, and I laughed, telling her she didn't understand my family. She was reassuring in her belief that with some work, I could start to set some limits.

As the weeks went on, I trusted her more. I decided to test the waters further by bringing up the most recent driving incident.

Since childhood, I was keenly aware of people's reactions and now could surmise what my clients were thinking, often before they could articulate it. I wanted to have that same intuition with my therapist. I thought I knew what she'd say—that I had a basic fear of heights and that perhaps I could try hypnosis. I watched the look on her face as I described my panic in the car, and revealed how and when it had happened before. I wondered if I had made a mistake by telling her because it became clear she was not going to let me off the hook so easily.

Reluctantly, I relented to the suggestion that I speak to a psychiatrist about the possibility of medication. A pill for anything other than physical pain was for people like my mother, those who were mentally ill, in my strong opinion. Was my therapist suggesting that I was suffering from some sort of psychotic behavior? I hated the discussion and had a hard time disguising my disdain for her during that negotiation. All this was foreign to me, and I didn't understand why my general doctor couldn't just prescribe something. My therapist was adamant that these types of medications should be under the directive of a specialist. I saw that she meant business, and I agreed, with reservations, to make an appointment.

Accepting that the anxiety disorder and panic attacks I was experiencing were not my fault did not come easy to me. I heard what my therapist said, understood that it was biochemical, but did not want to acknowledge it. I felt weak and vulnerable, and I thought I should be able to control it on my own. I hated the idea of medication. I hated even more that the therapist and psychiatrist compared it to my daily pill for blood pressure. David understood my hesitation, but saw what I was living with and felt it was worth a try. The psychiatrist did not want to discourage me any further by telling me the potential side effects; however, she shared one: "You might feel more anxious as we adjust your dose. I'm telling you because I don't want you to get frustrated and give up. I promise you I can help if you're willing to stick it out."

Being told she could help had me in tears once I was alone back in my car. I was touched by the compassion I was experiencing for the first time: women who seemingly cared for my well-being. I began to let down my guard and started to listen, not believing that I had all the answers.

My psychiatrist prescribed a daily dose of Lexapro and dissolvable Klonopin for on-demand use in the car or whenever I felt a panic attack coming on. True to her ominous warnings, I became extremely anxious with each Lexapro increase. For two to three days afterward, I felt like I was crawling out of my skin. I had to be alone in those moments and would find myself asking David not to speak or to leave the room. In total, it took almost six months to arrive at the correct dosage. I kept Klonopin tablets close by, and, to my surprise, they helped in the car. The panic didn't disappear, but it was more tolerable. I gained weight from the Lexapro, and the disgust I felt for my bloated body reached disproportionate levels, but I ignored the warnings about alcohol— cutting back was not an option.

My impatient and demanding demeanor did not tolerate stagnation. I looked at my weight gain as a setback but couldn't ignore the improvement from debilitating recurring anxiety. I took my daily dose religiously, and remained controlled about when and how to use Klonopin. At times it made me feel groggy, which only caused me to push harder. Just like a hangover, I took it as a personal challenge to work through any compromised feelings. I decided the best way to get a handle on my weight was to weigh myself daily. The number that appeared would dictate what I allowed myself to eat that day. It was a regimen I became loyal to, allowing me a sense of control.

Working in retail, my weight gain did not go unnoticed. Customers and friends alike commented on my appearance, causing my face to flush and revealing how self-conscious I was about what I, too, saw in the mirror. I had always been skinny or gawky. Now I looked bloated and chunky. David was incredibly sweet, telling me I looked much cuter with a little meat on my bones. I remained convinced he was lying and became silently more enraged every time he said it. I tried different ways of cutting my hair shorter, thinking it made me look thinner, but that drew attention to my ears.

Feeling determined to battle the repulsion I felt for my image, I scheduled an appointment to see a plastic surgeon. I needed to take action and figured after having suffered from having Dumbo ears my whole life I could at least tackle that. I hoped it would alleviate the shame that felt out of control. Hopeful and optimistic, I agreed to ear-pinning surgery. It would cost a small fortune, but as far as I was concerned, it was a small price to pay for something that would "fix" me. Besides, the doctor took credit cards, making it that much easier to justify. I convinced David and my therapist that this was just for me and that I was not doing it to please anyone else. I felt in my heart that this procedure would solve so much, and maybe even cure my anxiety disorder once and for all. I was desperate for any quick fix.

On my mom's birthday, I felt a panic attack coming on as soon as I saw my parents' car pull into the parking lot in front of my store. Without giving it much thought, I slipped a tablet under my tongue before they walked in the door.

Seeing them now felt ominously threatening, and I couldn't understand why. When I told my therapist about it, her expression betrayed her concern. I now understood that look and started to let some of my fears and doubts circulate in my mind and body. Something loomed under the surface, and I wanted to keep it from emerging and swallowing me whole.

Chapter Twelve

David and I went back to Levittown to celebrate Christmas. My solemn father, who immediately complained that our visit would be too short, greeted us at the door. I was exhausted and short-tempered after a busy retail season and weeks of decorating clients' houses. Spending time with my parents put me on edge even more, as my memory raced with thoughts of holidays growing up. The decorations, nativity, and stockings on the banister were all reminders of how volatile they had been. The smell of the annual gooey breakfast casserole coming from the kitchen made me sick to my stomach. I did not want to be there to experience the same routine.

Seeing gifts stacked high under the tree caused David and me to exchange a look, showing me that I was not alone in my frustration.

"Dad, this is way too much. I wish you hadn't done this."

He looked at me with an expression of hurt. "Don't take this joy away from me. It's all I have."

Agitated and not up to fighting a losing battle, I kept my mouth shut as David and I unwrapped gift baskets, socks, and unnecessary things for the house.

My mother's exorbitant bounty of presents remained unchanged since my childhood, and the sequence was the same. She laughed, cried, and feigned shock as she opened things that she had demanded. My parents looked at us blankly as they opened the few small gifts we brought them. They made it perfectly clear they did not share in our view that helping them out of debt and saving their home was enough for that year. Once alone with David, I apologized, embarrassed by their lack of gratitude and berated myself for putting him in that position.

By February, my father couldn't come up with the rent. He made excuses that things were slow at work and the cost of my mother's medications was astronomical. I believed that to be true, but also knew that he refused to take responsibility for anything that *was* within his control. When he came up short, he would include small notes explaining his dilemma. Every time I saw an extra piece of paper with a message scrawled across it, it reminded me of how much I regretted buying the house. I felt mocked—as if I had been made a fool—filling my head with the notion that I was trapped. I started to believe he was waiting for us to tell him he no longer had to pay rent. I sensed he expected it, but was still not desperate enough to demand it.

I wanted to distance myself from those nagging thoughts. At the end of the day, I would sometimes lose myself in music, staring into the fireplace with a martini in hand. When this worked, the evening would pass quietly as I drifted off to sleep on the sofa. I'd wake up in the middle of the night alone, finding David had gone to bed without me. On other nights, alcohol would have the opposite effect and draw me into melancholia. The tears that filled my eyes and fell across my face came from a deep sadness that I did not have access to. David often witnessed those outpourings of emotion but had become accustomed to them, chalking it up to my sensitivity. He had no way of knowing the dark thoughts that infiltrated those moments, thoughts that whispered a reprieve, a way out.

We had purchased a small stone house beautifully situated on a piece of land that offered complete privacy. It was a lifelong dream to own such a place. Yet the satisfaction for me was short-lived, as I immediately became impatient with the repairs that were needed. In an effort to project normality, I hosted a lot of dinners, driving home the point that everything was in order in our lives. I was uneasy in the evenings, and the dinner parties provided a labor-intensive task that would whisk away the hours.

David's mother, Camille, in my eyes, exemplified how to plan and serve a meal. Everything about her inspired me, and I quietly watched, wanting to emulate her. The Syrian tradition of having multiple main courses played into my need to comfort and please. Parties at our house always started with cocktails, and we made certain to have every option on hand. I'd often make them in advance, keeping them chilled in the refrigerator, gulping down the extra booze after I filled the glasses perfectly to their rims. Setting the table was a small feat unto itself, as I stared into the closet of vast table linens, selecting the perfect one for the occasion. I wanted those evenings to be flawless, and convinced myself that the better I made them, the better I'd feel about myself.

I got the strong sense I was making progress in therapy. I didn't dread going to see my therapist, and now that the Lexapro was doing what it was supposed to, my decrease in anxiety allowed me to absorb more of what she had to say. While I tried to refrain from showing that I was too vulnerable, I had shared enough about my family to warrant specific suggestions. I had even started employing some of them. I set new rules when my family visited the store, reiterating that this was my business and not my home. I witnessed my mother's tears after she felt I had scolded her and did my best to ignore the downturned smile my dad gave me, the look that caused me to apologize, even when I didn't know what I had done. Breaking old routines seemed to be one of my tasks at hand, and with my therapist's help I hoped I might be able to tackle some of them. I often left her office with reminders written on the back of her cards, such as "Don't invade my space." That kind of help was not something I ever asked for, but I began to trust her.

As my parents wedding anniversary approached, I decided that the years of sending gifts and money should come to an end. I couldn't stand that I had consistently indulged them and had preached the importance of curtailing unnecessary spending. Instead I sent a card, signing it from both David and me, without any cash included. The silence that followed did not come as a surprise, but went to work on my emotions. Eileen confirmed my suspicions when she told me how hurt my parents were that I did not send them money. They didn't understand how I could do that to them at a time when they felt they had so little. Without saying it, Eileen let me know that she too felt I had made a mistake.

Letting my guilt get the better of me, I called to arrange a time to visit them. I made no mention of the empty envelope and acted as if this was my plan all along. My father enthusiastically called out to my mother while I listened.

"Hey Karen, LJ wants to come home and treat us to lunch. How's next Saturday?"

I could envision the looks they were exchanging, feeling redeemed. I hated myself for doing that, but took what I considered the easy way out, not wanting to spend another session with my therapist combating the aftermath of disappointing my parents.

I was resolved to having a quick meal and returning as fast as I could. My mother was still soaking in her bath, so I went upstairs to use the bathroom. I hated the sick feeling that always crept up as I climbed those stairs. The house was showing its age, and I had a hard time absorbing the fact that it belonged to David and me. I peeked into my childhood bedroom, but seeing the worn carpeting and dirty walls depressed me. I crossed the hall into what had been my bedroom before I moved out. I stood in the doorway, shocked as I tried to grasp what I was seeing.

Between the slanted walls, they had installed a hanging bar from one end of the room to the other. The rod sagged from the weight of garments filling every inch. I saw all colors of two-piece matching outfits in pastel velour, the soft fabric meant to soothe my mother's physical ailments, with price tags still dangling from beneath the plastic wrappers. Woven holiday sweaters and multiple fleece jackets were flattened between long coats and hordes of denim jeans. The bed was covered in boxes with QVC printed on them in black, boldly announcing an addiction to shopping I hadn't fully realized. On the floor were piles of packages—kitchen gadgets, shoes, decorative pillows, and blankets—all stacked waiting to be opened. The village of stuffed animals had me perplexed, as I wondered if they were for my mother or the dog. The room was a warehouse of my mother's indulgences, illustrating a denial that made me tremble with anger and sadness.

"LJ, your mom's ready," my father called from the bottom of the stairs.

I made it through lunch without saying anything about what I'd seen, knowing the conversation would only cause an outburst from my mother and criticism from my father. As I reached for the check, my father said, "Thanks, landlord. You should do this more often."

I hated having to tell David what I had discovered. He had tolerated so much already, with my mother's moods and my father's insinuations, and I couldn't help but wonder if this would be his last straw of tolerance. When I saw him face to face, he recognized something was wrong.

"How'd it go?"

I was shaken, but he listened without judgment. Once again, he found a way to separate me from my family, something I could not do.

"You're going to have to do something."

I agreed, and began to think about the best way to tackle this new dilemma.

With the help of my therapist, I crafted a carefully worded email. My father was new to using a computer, and my mother wanted nothing to do with them, believing they were evil. Putting my concerns in writing was a way for me to say what I needed to without the hindrance of his expressions or standard responses that pulled me into the mire of guilt. A way to be direct without any of the standard Ruhl family blurred lines. I addressed our concerns for their spending, and his inability to consistently send us the money he owed. I needed to remind him that this was not a gift, but rather a solution that we had hoped would work. I felt accomplished that I had tackled the situation head on and thanked my therapist for the guidance.

Within a few days, I received a response. My father reminded me what a good person he was, and reiterated that he never said no to my suffering mother, or to me whenever I had asked for something. They had been put off by my email and felt it was not my place to tell them what they could and couldn't spend money on. He did not believe this new round of debt was his fault, and I needed to take the good with the bad, love him as he was.

Reading his words made my face flush, and I felt catapulted back to being a young boy in his garden, listening to his musings on how things "should" be between father and son. His reminding me that he had not been able to refuse me made my head spin with confusion. I felt panicked and unsteady, and I couldn't catch my breath.

I walked out to get some air on our front porch. David said something to me as I passed, but I continued on, not hearing him. Seeing that I was unresponsive, he followed. Sweat covered my body, and my mouth went dry. I could not stop shaking, and as he got closer I started to cry, sinking down to a crouching position on the floor.

He put his hand on my shoulder, asking, "What is it? Are you okay?" I could only shake my head no. He leaned in to hug me, but I remained motionless, rigid in his arms as my sobs intensified.

Sorrow gripped me by the ankles, threatening to pull me underground. I had no way to fight back and surrendered to David. I sobbed and repeated "No, no, no." He held me close, telling me it would be okay, but it was not okay—and we both knew it.

"I think we should call your therapist," he quietly suggested, but I answered that she was away. "Surely there's an answering service or something. I'll get the phone."

I felt the cool air against my damp skin and shivered, sitting defenseless until he returned. Within an hour, the psychiatrist on call phoned me back.

I explained as best I could the events that led up to that moment, ending with reading my father's email. Embarrassed, I admitted that I thought something bad was about to happen to me.

"I'm not sure what to do. I feel like I'm going crazy."

Her tone became assertive as she made her suggestion. "Larry, I am going to ask you to not have further contact with your family until you see your therapist. Is that something you can commit to?"

I agreed and shared with David what she'd said, but the look of concern remained on his face.

I took a walk along the edge of our pond, looking at the reflection of the tree branches in the rippling water. My mind whirled with the idea of ending my life. I sat on the edge of the dock and took comfort in knowing I would never have to revisit any of those childhood feelings, if I chose that. This was a solution, an exit strategy, and I had to keep it close by from now on. I was good at keeping secrets, and adding this one offered me comfort.

My therapist scheduled a phone session with me immediately upon her return, not waiting to see me in person. I recounted the reaction I had to reading my father's email and the sadness and darkness that followed. I could not cleanse the filth inside of me, and I was distraught and hopeless. I did not believe that whatever was happening was going to leave anytime soon. I kept my thoughts of ending my life to myself. If I was going to succumb to silence, I did not want to have someone to talk me out of it.

It was perfectly clear that I needed to at least temporarily sever the relationship with my parents. I agreed with her that this was the right tactic.

So much of this felt old, and as I replayed the email over and over in my head, I felt the self-hate that haunted me in my childhood. I wanted to understand, to rationalize it. My therapist reassured me it was okay to be confused.

"This is something that will take time. Can you trust in the process and stick it out?

I agreed, but secretly did not know.

With David and my therapist supporting me, I wrote an email to my parents, looping Eileen in, explaining that I would need a complete break from communication. Admitting that much of my childhood brought me shame, grief, and anger felt provocative but honest. I apologized for not living up to my commitment to come home to care for my mother after her imminent knee surgery. This filled me with fear, knowing how hurt she'd be. It ate away at me at night, and I wondered if my sister and father could rise to the occasion and do for her what I would do.

In his response, my father said if I did not come home, my mother would no longer have anything to do with me. I instinctively knew that was no exaggeration.

I found it disturbing to feel guilty about my father. His words from two decades earlier rang through my ears: "Would you miss me if I killed myself?"

I was sick to my stomach with worry one minute, and filled with rage the next. I questioned if I could live with the responsibility if he did commit suicide. I tried to grasp onto the fact that I was no longer a child, but I couldn't shake the sensation that I was still under his control. He did not let up, sending emails that told me he understood this was hard for me, but this was hard on him too. He said he was the one who always tried to fix our family problems, but he couldn't possibly fix something he didn't understand.

Reaching deep into the past, I tried to recall what he meant by fixing our family problems. I thought of the fights between my parents and realized how little he had actually done to protect us. It was painful to recall those images, and the idea that he felt he had done something to "fix" it showed me how delusional he was.

I forwarded every correspondence to my therapist and stayed in constant touch, writing to her between my twice-a-week office visits.

My father asked me to reconsider coming home for my mother's operation, explaining that if we had time alone, father and son, we could work things out. Reading those words made my hands tremble. I did not know what to do with the memories that infiltrated my consciousness. I thought of him saying those exact words to me as a boy. I stood and paced the bedroom trying to figure out what to do. I needed desperately to put it all out of my mind.

"Ready for a martini?" I called out to David.

I pulled the vodka from the freezer and poured a tumbler full for myself before mixing two perfect cocktails. I tilted my head back and downed the contents in two quick intervals. The slow burn in my throat and chest warmed and comforted me, offering me a reprieve. Feeling the numbing effect across my body, I grounded my feet onto the floor and steadied my hands. *You're okay.* I caught my reflection in the window. I rinsed the glass and put it away, hiding evidence of my extra indulgence. As David walked in, we toasted each other and settled into the evening. Surrendering to the effects of the alcohol, I drifted into unconsciousness.

═════════

Eileen's biggest concern was how this would affect my relationship with her daughter. I reassured her we could help her understand. What unnerved me was how quickly Eileen accepted my need to cut ties with my parents. She never asked why.

My main focus was to get through the days without falling apart, despite feeling completely irrational. I paced a lot: at the shop, at home, on the street. I had to keep moving. My therapist had encouraged me to write more frequently. I worried that my mother or someone else would discover what I documented and somehow use it against me, causing me even more shame and embarrassment. Still, I pushed myself to write as often as I could tolerate it. I could not ignore the relief I felt as I purged words, thoughts, and actions onto my computer screen or in a journal.

I was the keeper of all our family memorabilia. Boxes of photos, documents, holiday decorations, and letters haunted me from their hiding places in the attic and basement. My therapist was willing to dedicate an afternoon to working with me, so I hauled everything into her office to sort through it. I talked about the irony of being the one to have such things, having rescued many of them from the trash after my mother attempted to rid herself of them in fits of rage. Stopping to look at a picture of my father from when I was a young boy, I handed it to her and said, "This one makes me sick."

She stared back at me as I continued, "He's trying to look sexy."

I saw my father looking at me from the other side of the camera, telling me to join him under the blanket. *I'll scratch your back. Come on, we'll have some of our father-son time.*

The words rang through my ears as if they had just happened.

Excusing myself, I went into the bathroom to splash some water on my face.

I heard myself say "sexy," and panic rose up into my throat. I wished I hadn't said it, but it was too late; she had heard me and now it was there, hovering in the space between us.

———

That Christmas would be the first without my parents. I sent them an email wishing them a good holiday and explained that I needed more time, and I loved them. When it came to my mother, I worried. I missed her despite her complete silence, and I felt concerned for her state of mind. Eileen was willing to travel to me just after Christmas, a new tradition, to create a sense of normalcy for my niece. When they arrived, my niece gave me a hug and whispered in my ear, "That's from Pap-Pap."

Disgusted, I wanted to scream at her to never do that again. I hated how he was trying to get to me through an innocent girl.

The dark mysteries stirring in my memory had me constantly questioning myself, asking how it was possible. *How could he have done these things to me?*

The push of what I understood to be true in my heart against my desire to not believe it dragged me down.

Eileen remained silent and accepting. She did not ask questions, but rather obliged my need for distance from my parents. My feelings for my sister confused me, but to maintain a relationship with my only niece, I had to find a way to tolerate them.

I drank my way through the evenings.

The sadness and despair were relentless, and I resorted to the only reliable tool I had. I pushed my way through gut-churning hangovers to prove I was not drinking too much.

More than ever, I believed if I stopped running I would fall apart and never recover. I ran my business thoroughly, never letting on I was suffering. I cooked and played house flawlessly to disguise my pain and confusion. David did not ask questions. This came as a relief and a burden. I had learned how to make his naivety work in my favor, and it was easy to conceal my suicidal thoughts and selfish motives. It was too painful to imagine his lack of inquiry meant a lack of interest. Instead, I manipulated our lives to get what I needed. My intense desire to feel in control got me through the day.

Whenever I checked my email and saw my father's name, if I wasn't alone or near a drink, I would not read it. My reactions to his emails were unreliable, varying from extreme anger to extreme emotion.

As I read his words, *I'm just numb all over. One moment I want to grab you and beat the shit out of you, and the next I want to hold you to show you how much I love you,* I became disgusted.

Now there was no mistaking how he had shown me how much he loved me.

Now those ways were coming back to me, destabilizing me and making me try to shut them out at any cost.

Chapter Thirteen

The woman occupying my studio apartment in Manhattan was quiet and private, the perfect tenant. When she called to tell me it was time for her to move on, I seized the opportunity to start using it again. David had little need or desire to be back in the city, but I cited the list of reasons why it was a smart decision: meeting clients, shopping for projects, and the added benefit of saving money by no longer staying in hotel rooms.

My mind was often clouded, as snapshots of my childhood bounced in and out. Trying to make sense of it kept me constantly on edge, and I struggled to feel safe. I was too afraid to admit it, even to myself, but David and I were hitting some rough terrain. We both had busy professional lives, but I wanted more from him. He had always been incredibly good at self-care, making his needs a priority—and my resentment toward that behavior intensified. I hated that on a slow day he could easily stay in bed reading a book or sleeping. I wanted and expected him to jump in and offer help with a business that was half his. I became more hyper-vigilant than ever, and in contrast, he seemed to retract and slow down.

The apartment offered me an escape from him and my responsibilities. I envisioned it as my secret getaway, a way to soothe my conflicted state of mind. I could lose myself in a few cocktails without raising any eyebrows. Nothing put me more at ease than drinking alone.

I attempted to bury myself in the lives of my clients. I felt in control as I made decisions for them, to beautify their homes. Choosing paint colors, fabrics, and furnishings became as important to me as brushing my teeth, and when engaged that way, I could deflect from feeling stained. Creating beauty allowed me a place to put my mind at temporary rest from feeling like a moving target. Sadness waited patiently to lure me into a dark place if I stopped moving.

My therapy sessions took on a heightened intensity. Saying out loud what I remembered from my pre-teen years felt impossible. I worried that my therapist wouldn't believe me, but many of my memories were vivid.

There was no mistaking the truths that were emerging.

I left the store for an hour twice a week for sessions where I alternated between sadness and discouraging frustration, plaguing me and weighing me down. Her "slower is faster" plan offered little relief. It made sense, that I could not force a lifetime of damaging behavior to resolve all at once, but sitting in the discomfort was agonizing.

During a particularly intense session, she suggested that when I was ready, I should write out everything I could recall as of that day, adding things as they emerged. Days later, I created a bulleted list of what I felt ready to face.

My father's game of tickling my back with a dinner fork and spelling out words for me to guess. If I got the answer right, he'd pull me in close, kiss my neck, and tell me what a good boy I was. If I got it wrong, he'd go slower, sliding himself up tight against me as I lay face down.

I wrote about his arousal, remembering it as recently as when I signed the papers on the house, that father-son moment in the hallway. I thought about his hands on my shoulders, back, and backside when I was barely a teen, but I couldn't discern what felt normal and what went too far. I knew when I had a migraine I had asked him to massage my shoulders. Now I questioned whether I had encouraged him and felt my face flush with disgust. The confusion made me angry, and I turned that anger inward. I kept my focus on exactly what I knew and wrote out as many details as I could: the blanket he used to cover us, the sweat pants he wore, the shag carpeting of the living room floor underneath me.

My nights were restless, and I often woke up drenched in sweat. The experience with my mother's friend's son, Robert, pounded at my brain. As I recalled him forcing himself into my mouth, I suddenly knew it was not the first time that was done to me.

I got out of bed and walked through the house, panic surging in my chest.

"You okay?"

Startled, I turned to find David, looking sleepy.

"Couldn't sleep, but I'm good. I'll be up in a minute."

He kissed me on the forehead, but I remained still, unable to return the gesture. When I got back into bed, I stared at the ceiling, letting the disgust I felt for myself sink in. I swallowed an Ativan, the recent addition to my cache of anti-anxiety medications, before closing my eyes.

I was quickly losing interest in sex with David. It was impossible not to think of my father when I saw David in the bathroom, towel wrapped around his waist. His bare chest made my stomach churn, and I had to avert my eyes, making sure he didn't notice. I pulled away from what had been a standard in our relationship, long embraces. I loved him but felt repulsed by him.

As I tried to maintain my composure, I was determined I needed to take action, to figure out some things on my own. I thought I could rush the process, despite my therapist's adamant proclamations otherwise. Angry, I'd ask myself if she was telling me this to keep me paying her fee. "Slower is faster" reverberated in my head as I combatted it with thoughts of "fuck you." I thought ripping the bandage off quickly was the best option.

The city apartment offered me total seclusion to sort through my raging thoughts. Conflicts about my sexuality reemerged, and I focused on the feelings that stirred around David. I had no idea what felt safe, let alone enjoyable. I obsessed over my previous experiences of getting massages from men. I flashed back to that first time, of getting aroused, and the shame that set in so quickly. I sensed it was connected to what had happened, but I couldn't figure out how. Determined to get answers, I turned to Craigslist.

I drank enough to soften my edges and tame my nerves as I typed "massage" into the search field under "Men for Men," not knowing what to expect. The page filled in an instant with ads. I read multiple posts, feeling disgusted by those that clearly offered sex, but optimistic at the "legitimate" ones.

I believed if I could get through a massage with a man and not get aroused, then somehow what happened to me wasn't my fault. I felt a wave of guilt come over me because I was somehow betraying David, but desperation and the effects of vodka took over as I narrowed down my choices.

I selected a tall, Hispanic guy who was younger than me by a few years. I chose him in part because, unlike so many of the others, he did not show naked photos, out of personal "discretion." This impressed me as I thought about my own privacy. I paced the apartment waiting for him. I slammed back two more shots to calm my nerves, hoping I wouldn't chicken out. I was already worried about what *he* would think.

I buzzed him in and listened carefully for his footsteps as he made his way up to the fourth floor. Katherine flashed into my thoughts, as did the sound of her feet on the tile floor as she left me in the apartment, and I instantly felt ashamed of what I was about to do.

The rap on the door jolted me into awareness, and opening it swiftly, I came face to face with Carlos, a tall, well-built, decent-looking guy. The most important aspect of his appearance was that he looked nothing like my father or David. In my hazy state, I asked him in.

He asked if I was particularly tense in any part of my body. I didn't get the sense he was trained, but went along with the charade anyway. My shoulders and back were a constant source of pain and tension, and I relayed that to him, hoping I might actually get something out of this experiment. He instructed me to remove my clothes and lay face down on the bed. As I readied myself, he disappeared into the bathroom.

When I found myself lying there, naked and vulnerable, it suddenly occurred to me I might be putting myself at risk inviting a stranger into my apartment. My stomach knotted with doubt, but it was too late as I heard the toilet flush and the bathroom door open.

He had a good, firm touch and worked out the tension in my neck, down my shoulders, and into my lower back. I tingled all over feeling his hands work on me, trying not to let my thoughts wander beyond that present moment. I started to feel nervous as he finished my feet, dreading him asking me to turn over. Hearing him say it, I took comfort in the fact that I had not gotten aroused up until that point.

As I rolled onto my back, I pulled the blanket over me, covering myself. He laughed and asked me if I was embarrassed. My face flushed, and I nodded yes.

"Don't be. I'll relax you." His kindness surprised me, and I wanted to cry. My arousal became unavoidable, but instead of fleeing the bed, I stayed there, acting as if it wasn't happening, remaining silent. I wanted to touch him, to see if he was aroused too, but I was afraid to move, afraid to make contact. I became restless and started to stretch out whichever limbs he wasn't focusing on. His hand moved across my torso and rested on my erection. "Want me to take care of that for you?"

My own sense of calm caught me by surprise. "No thanks. Maybe next time."

Our eyes met and he smiled as he went back into the bathroom. I stood, putting my underwear back on, and pulled out the hundred dollars from the hiding place I had tucked it into.

I waited until I heard the slam of the door to the street before sitting back down.

I had lost my own contest and was disappointed. But I felt an odd sense of relief that I had been attracted to him, taking it as a sign that I had not lost a sense of desire. I wondered if he was aroused too and found me attractive. My conflicted emotions and feelings felt like a firestorm. I wanted to feel attractive and be attracted to other men, but I also ridiculed myself for showing the weakness of arousal.

I tried to make sense of my father's erections and his smothering affection and attention. It felt crazy to think I could have encouraged him, yet I couldn't shake that question. But the longer I let myself ruminate on the rituals of my childhood, the clearer they became.

Going to the apartment became a regular habit. I let myself continue my experiments with massages and drifting into my dark thoughts. As far as David and my employees were concerned, I was busy with clients. I was desperate for silence and solitude, allowing only carefully chosen visitors to come into my space, my discernment increasing with each new experience.

When I imagined ending my life, I considered many factors: my own fear of blood, concerns that I wouldn't do it correctly and wind up suffering in some incapacitated state, or that I would fail and get caught, facing the shame of complete failure. I saw a botched suicide attempt as the ultimate fuck up. Shooting myself seemed too gruesome, and I did not want to put David through that. Hanging became much more appealing, as I would be discovered in one piece.

But the idea that seduced me most, and had me planning and plotting discreetly, was to ingest enough pills to do the job peacefully and quickly.

I created a hiding place in a small antique box tucked into the far reaches of the apartment closet. Here, I accumulated Ativan and Klonopin tablets. On each trip to the city, I left two or three of each, thinking by the time I was ready, there would be enough of a stash to thoroughly sedate me after I swallowed the bottle of blood pressure pills I'd bring along. The slow gas leak in the oven would come in handy, and I kept plastic from dry cleaning under the kitchen sink, to cover my face and mouth as an extra precaution. Back at home within my routine, I hated that summer was fast approaching.

I didn't understand why the season had such an awful impact on me, but now it seemed even more unsettling to face summer parties with shirtless men. What had once been a source of sexual energy and attraction now filled me with dread. Though I no longer got panic attacks, the medication fending them off with success, I still felt anxious, especially in large groups or at parties. The summer also produced sweat, which along with any body odor, I found intolerable.

I flashed back to my father in his bathtub, sweat on his forehead, and the smell of him after work in the summer heat, and was so nauseated I could barely breathe.

I was unbalanced but yearned to feel grounded. I was able to get up the courage to share some of this with my therapist, but the remainder I kept tucked away in my growing cache of secrets.

After a particularly bad trip to the city that saw me, in my drunken state, hiring multiple masseurs over the course of two nights, my therapist asked more detailed questions about my activities. Feeling weak from a sinister hangover and tired of bearing the weight of uncertainty, I confessed that I had been slipping into a dark place when

I was there. I spoke of my attempts to feel normal by hiring men to give me massages, and at last, confided in her that I had been keeping a stash of pills.

To my surprise, she did not get angry or show panic in any way. I sensed she was concerned, and that feeling was cemented when she asked for the address of the apartment, and confirmation that she had the correct contact information for David.

I would not admit it to her, but I felt relieved despite telling myself that if I decided to kill myself, none of those things would matter. It was part of my plan to make sure that I had time to do it properly without the risk of interruption or early discovery.

During this chaotic misery, I was at the height of my design business. I was earning more than ever, and the contrast to what was happening internally and what I outwardly projected was stark.

I used my income to further numb myself with layers of padding to help keep me protected. I dined at the best restaurants, taking friends and employees for long nights out, whisking away the bill when it arrived without thought. I spent money on things for the house and for my dinner parties that would elevate them to a new level, making sure there was no room for blight, in my home or in me.

The more money I took in and subsequently spent, the less stained and disgusting I felt. Like drinking, the pull to consume more enmeshed itself in every area of my life. I hated that nothing seemed to fill the void in my chest, but would not give up trying to find what would.

The dichotomy of my existence was staggering. I often felt I was hanging on by a thread, even when I sat through lavish evenings of cocktails, dinner, and after-hours clubs. It was the only way I felt I could manage getting through the days and weeks ahead.

David and I went to Rome to commemorate ten years together. On our second night there, we indulged in a magnificent restaurant to honor our relationship. After our second round of cocktails, I was anxious about being alone with him, and I struggled to feel romantic. I worried this might happen before we left, but I brushed my concerns aside, thinking I'd find a way to work through it. Sitting across from him in this beautiful setting, my fears materialized.

Feeling tense, I took this opportunity to berate him. I blindsided him with my observations of how obnoxious he was, and how his arrogance filled me with anger every time he walked through the door. He returned the fire by citing just how demanding I had become, saying it was impossible to satisfy me. Our language and tone intensified, and I gathered momentum, feeling I was airing issues that were justified.

Exasperated by my belligerence, David finally left the restaurant. I caught his reflection in the window, and as I saw him out on the street, I smirked, feeling victorious. I lifted my martini in a mock toast and downed the balance in one gulp.

When we got back home, we focused on our individual lives, not wanting to revisit or acknowledge the things we said to each other. The great divide grew, but we distracted ourselves. We had friends over often, relying on one of our favorite pastimes, drinking. David could easily leave a cocktail unfinished when he felt he had had enough. I didn't understand that, and when I cleared away the glasses, I downed whatever was left in his glass before putting it in the sink. How could he possibly be so wasteful?

I resumed my city trips with vigor, losing myself in the mania of questionable routines. I was running on empty. As I pushed myself to maintain the pace I had established, I tried to hide the effect it was having on me.

My nights in the city became like those at home, as I stared into the darkness thinking someone was going to break in and hurt me. I couldn't combat the on-edge feelings I experienced when I heard someone in the hall, or when a noise rattled outside the window. I took more Ativan and washed it down with booze, but stayed awake, terrified.

After one sleepless night, I got up early, feeling jittery. I walked quickly to the garage to retrieve my car and head back north. I had to get out of the apartment. As I drove up the east side of Manhattan, I felt the wave of sadness from the night before revisit my chest. By the time I crossed the bridge exiting the city, I had drifted into dark thoughts of ending my life.

No one will know. This is your chance.

I wasn't expected home until the afternoon, and had another day before I was scheduled to see my therapist. My heart raced as I ran through my checklist of necessary tools, and I felt satisfied that everything was in place back in the apartment. I merged into traffic and steadied my hands on the steering wheel.

My eyes filled with tears.

I pulled off onto the shoulder of the highway. As cars raced past, I fell into deep sobs, losing control of my emotions. I looked at myself in the mirror, saying out loud "You're pathetic."

I continued out of the city.

The next day, I used my session as confession. I recounted what had happened and ratted myself out, divulging the steps I had taken to plan my suicide. I was angry and felt stupid. My therapist listened with compassion, but as our time came to a close, she asked that David join us at our next scheduled time.

I knew if I were going to tackle what had been filling my brain, I'd have to come clean with David. This was it.

As he joined in my next session, he could not disguise his anger and frustration. The weight of not being privy to what I was silently holding onto left him feeling exasperated. But as he listened to what I was able to admit, his concern overruled his senses, and he fought back tears. I felt embarrassed and defeated as I tried to absorb his kindness.

Anxiety fueled my relentless need for motion, but I found myself inexplicably slowed, unable to move. The fact that I had succumbed to depression was undeniable, despite my efforts to prove that I could tackle it through nonstop work and drinking. The weeks that followed were challenging.

I could not return to the city, having broken a trust with both David and my therapist. Despite my assurances, they outright asked me not to go. I hated being told what to do, but I was not yet sure I could trust myself.

I felt the darkness dissipate as yet another medication worked its magic. In moments alone, I thought back to that drive home and what ran through my mind, frightened by how out of control I felt.

In my efforts to bulldoze my way through my emotional unraveling, I had been in talks to open a design studio and showroom in the city. That year the economy tanked, and everything came to a standstill. It became abundantly clear that pursuing a deeper commitment to the city was not advisable, and I shelved those plans and focused on the clients I had who were unaffected by the financial crisis.

In an uncanny coincidence of timing, David and I received a certified letter from the owner of the apartment building. In detail, it listed the names of the illegal tenants I had rented to over the years. I was losing the lease and would have to vacate by year's end. There was no way to argue or fight to keep it.

David and I looked at it as a blessing in disguise. I had not been back since the experience on the highway, still feeling the residual fear it produced. David stepped in and handled all the logistics, keeping me from any further interaction. When the boxes arrived with all the apartment contents, I tucked them unopened into storage, not ready to revisit any part of it.

Chapter Fourteen

My father continued his attempts to maintain contact, sending emails addressing problems with the house, and mailing cards for our birthdays, Christmas, Easter, and the anniversary of the store's opening. Seeing his handwriting on an envelope filled me with an uneasy disgust. I no longer opened any of them, choosing to hand them over to my therapist. My father's language was consistently disturbing, expressing his desire to hold me close and signing off with "my love now and forever." He signed my mother's name along with his, but aside from that, she remained silent and detached.

The cards disappeared at the hands of my therapist, who shredded them, taking the responsibility from me. David remained at my side, not asking for details, but he could tell when I had received some sort of correspondence. On rare occasions, my father would leave a message on the answering machine at the store, instilling complete panic in me as I rushed to hit the erase button. Hearing his voice felt like an invasion, and I tried to clear my head of his words: "Hi, Son. Just wanted to say that I love you."

In one of his emails, my father pressed me for answers, wanting to know if I were making any progress in sorting things out.

I decided to confront him in writing about his arousal while he and I watched television, moments just between us, branded in my memory. I wanted to break my silence with clarity, detailing one of the "games" he played. I wrote about his tickling my back under the fleece blanket—the one with the two-tone brown horse—on the living room floor and his erection pushing up against me. The anger stirred as I wrote out what I needed to say, being careful to not lead myself into one of his guilt entrapments.

He responded by asking where this was all coming from. He said if I thought he had gotten aroused, I really had a problem. He also shared a detail that made me wince. He said I had taken something his mother did to relax him as a child and turned it into something disgusting.

What exactly had she done to him?

He went on to say I had locked all of this in my brain without giving him the opportunity to explain, and he reminded me we *all* had to deal with the dynamics of our family, not just me.

My anger intensified. He was speaking to me as an equal counterpart and not his son. He tried to convince me I was mistaken, that I had "locked" things in my brain that did not happen.

Yes, they happened, and so did many other things he asked me to keep private.

I flashed back to those conversations as a young boy, when he relied on me as his confidant.

Was I wrong to think that as his child it wasn't my job to figure things out for him or my mother? He failed at protecting us from our mother, and now he still spoke to me as if this was a burden we were meant to share. The fact that he was speaking the same language all those years later made my jaw clench, as I thought about how delusional he was.

He ended by saying he wished he and I could have worked things out together, but he was happy I moved on to a better life for myself. The email closed with, "Even though you don't believe me, I wouldn't do anything to intentionally hurt you, and that's the truth whether you want to believe it or not."

His denial became more transparent than ever before.

Writing him using the words *arousal, tickling,* and *blanket* flooded me with thoughts of our time together.

The hunting trips, lying next to me in bed, and his hands on me in the car when I went with him to work filled me with yet more disgust and fear.

After a therapy session where I recounted more details of oral sex with him as a young boy, I wondered how to leave her office and resume normality back in the shop, confronting the constant stream of folks in and out the front door. We ended our session the way we always had any time it was particularly raw and disturbing: checking to be certain that I felt safe and grounded, though rattled.

As I got in my car, I locked my door—something I never thought to do on any other day. My chest pounded as I glanced in the back seat to make certain no one was there. Pulling onto the highway, I wondered if the car in my rearview mirror was following me.

As I walked in the front door fear consumed me, and I became convinced my father was coming to get me. Terrified, I turned off the lights and put the "Closed" sign up. I watched over my shoulder as I returned to my car and drove home, doors locked, staring straight ahead. I resorted to a coping strategy that would sometimes soothe my nerves, increasing the volume on a song I replayed over and over again, the car vibrating from the decibel level of the speakers. Turning onto the side road that led to our house, I decreased the volume and phoned David.

Answering with our standard end-of-the-day greeting he said, "Vodka or gin?"

"Gin, please. It's been a long day."

Fear of being called crazy, like my mother, kept me from telling David the truth about what consumed me in moments alone. Instead, I became more distant, keeping personal details to a minimum. His glazed-over looks illustrated he could only absorb so much anyway, and I did not want to burden him with the ugliness of what I was tackling.

He had a tendency to be dismissive, and I couldn't handle that behavior when it came to this. He often half-listened as he looked at his mail or emails. The anger in my chest at feeling secondary forced me into deeper silence. While I battled the hideous fragments of truth as they emerged, David and I were drifting even further away from each other. I wondered if he felt it too.

My need for solitude felt genuine. I started to hate the constant interaction with people that retail demanded, feeling as though I had no escape. The stream of comments about my appearance grated on my nerves and did little to help my already deteriorated self-esteem.

Settling into the reprieve of privacy in one of the only places I could find it, at home in the bathroom, isolation now turned against me as it screamed out how I really felt about myself.

I tried to remove the filth I believed covered my body. I stood in the hottest shower I could tolerate, steam seeping out under the door, until my fingers were wrinkled from the moist heat. I scrubbed my body raw using the scouring sponge I had slipped into the pocket of my bathrobe from the kitchen sink. Starting at my feet, I didn't leave a patch of skin untouched by the abrasive surface that I was convinced would help to remove my stains if I worked diligently. I scrubbed and scrubbed, causing my skin to become raw in places, blood trickling down into the drain. Stepping out of the shower, I'd pat myself gingerly with a towel, not wanting to leave any traces of blood for David to question.

Catching my reflection in the mirror caused me to stop and stare. I could not deny the fact that I looked like my dad, a truth that lead me to admonish the puffy face that stared back at me, reminding me I was disgusting and fat. Inheriting his appearance was the worst kind of joke—the ultimate *fuck you* in my efforts to separate from him.

I felt so worthless and tainted, I was sure I repulsed others just with my close proximity. I became certain that others saw what I saw, a disgusting and soiled boy. That same boy who looked in the mirror at home in Levittown and wondered if he should dare to put on his mother's lipstick—the faggot then and still now.

———

Nights were restless, my combination of booze and anti-anxiety pills betraying me as I jolted up in bed from fractured sleep, covered in sweat and trembling with fear that someone was in the house. My hand gripping David's shoulder made him sit up, asking if I was okay.

"I think someone is in the house," I'd whisper, and he'd listen with me. David would put me at ease, often going downstairs to investigate, kissing me on the forehead before returning to sleep.

His kindness was the only thing that allowed me to feel safe in my own home; however, in a complete contradiction, I became more detached from him sexually. I could not separate thinking of what my father had done to me from the man who shared my life now.

Rejecting him made me feel guilty and trapped, and I saw no way out of it. My therapist helped me understand how normal, even expected, this was, but that didn't help. The day-to-day agony I felt just being in the same room with him consumed me.

I turned to books on sexual abuse, scanning the pages, looking for ways to conquer my feelings, but there was no quick fix, no easy way out. I was saying those two words aloud to myself now. *Sexual abuse.*

At a summer birthday party filled with clients and friends, David and I parted ways as we socialized with different groups, not allowing ourselves to overlap. I refilled my plastic cup, maintaining a constant level of a spiked fruity drink, accepting refills every time they were offered. My inhibitions softening, I allowed myself to be lured into the pool, something I'd sworn off as the pounds had increased. Feeling the warmth of the alcohol swirl in my head, I stripped down to my briefs, quickly sliding my way in, knees bent to conceal my chest. The men in the pool intimidated me with their buff bodies and glaring self-confidence.

This was out of character for me, the reserved shopkeeper who excelled at keeping up appearances. I joined in the fun, tossing a beach ball around, forcing laughter, catching David's stare from the corner of my eye.

Someone splashed water in my direction, and returning the gesture, the instigator took my arm, lifting me out of the water, tossing me to the middle of the pool.

"It's more fun to toss Larry around," he yelled out childishly.

With that, all eyes were on us, and I loved the attention, laughing, flirting, and grabbing on to the necks of the men who surrounded me. David stood at the edge, announcing it was time to go home.

"Not yet. I'm their volleyball."

The game was quickly changing course.

As the hunkiest of the men caught me, he held me close as he announced, "Game over, I won the prize."

He wrapped his arms even tighter around my waist. "Did you have fun?"

I nodded sheepishly. He offered me a sip of his cocktail, holding me as he put the cup to my lips. His erection was apparent, and I recognized the familiarity of being in a man's arms, held too close, not sure if I'd be able to catch my next breath.

I was caught up in a swirl of feelings. I felt trapped in the intoxicating feeling of another man's affections. I felt defiant and lost any sense of concern for who might be watching me, let alone my partner.

"Hey Larry, I think you need to check on David," someone interrupted from the sidelines, annoying me.

I felt young, like I had done something terrible and had to face the disciplinarian. As I drove home alone, along the windy roads, nausea swirling in my stomach, I was grateful David and I had arrived in separate cars. When I got home, David was in a chair facing the door, staring at me with disdain.

"What is it? What's wrong?" I asked.

"I can't talk about it now."

I hated that, once again, he was going silent. "Just say it, David. Say what's on your fucking mind for once."

My temper flared. I wanted him to be honest, be a man about what was bothering him. To my surprise, he responded.

"You were disgusting being tossed around like that. Like some whore."

My hands trembled with rage. Without a word, I reached for a glass of water, my mouth feeling pasty and dry at the same time.

"Just do it, Lar. I can see you want to, so just do it!"

Barely waiting for him to finish, I threw the glass of water in his face, giving in to the anger that pressed me to do much worse.

Restless in my therapist's office, I unleashed the list of reasons why it was time for me to end my relationship with David.

She had heard my doubts before, but now I did not want to sustain her assertions that we could find a way to work through it. In addition to my lack of sexual attraction, I finally admitted that David's insensitivity had worn me down. He soaked up the nurturing things I did without a second thought, such as bringing him coffee in bed every morning and making sure I left the lights on for him when he was out late. These small gestures were things he was incapable of returning. When I arrived home in a rainstorm to find the door locked, and lights off, the sadness I felt for being forgotten consumed me, and I had a hard time looking at him.

Asking him to do those things was out of the question; I wanted him to do them on his own, to anticipate them as I did for him.

But what I found hardest to confess was that I had fantasies about life without him. I imagined his sudden death and what would follow. In my illusion, I felt free, envisioning this enormous pressure lifted, and I no longer had to keep myself together and find a way to work through all of this for anyone's benefit but mine. I could travel freely and be as anonymous as I wanted to be, moving from town to town. In my hypothetical thinking, the burden of being a couple was lifted from me. The decision I felt forced to make was a difficult one.

Was I willing to flex enough muscle to end it while we were both alive? I wasn't sure I could do it, preferring to become consumed with the idea that he left me either by his demise or a decision on his own. Either fantasy came to me as a relief. My demise wasn't part of this fantasy.

My therapist suggested that before either of us broached the subject of ending our relationship, we should consider seeing a couple's therapist. I was agitated, thinking of yet another therapist in our lives. David had his; I had mine. A third struck me as excessive and annoying, but I couldn't deny the point she was driving home.

"You really have nothing to lose. At least this way if you do decide to put an end to it, you'll both know that you gave it everything you could."

We were both emotionally drained, but trusted that if nothing else, we would learn more about ourselves, good or bad.

But meeting Madeline put much of our uncertainty to rest, as we were drawn in by her energy and forthrightness, and began the daunting process of laying out our scenario to her.

We sat through those early sessions exploring what was on the surface: My feelings that David always put himself first, unaware what was going on around him, and his refusal to stand up for himself, to authority, and to me. His cockiness was infuriating, and I often felt alone in picking up the pieces of the feelings he had bruised. The effects of his background, his family dynamics, and upbringing entered the picture—precarious territory to navigate—making it clear to me how imperative it was to have this therapist in front of us, our referee and our champion.

In turn, I could not deny David's grievances. I had lied, kept secrets, kept him on edge with my thoughts of suicide and frequent emotional breakdowns. When he admitted that he found the rifle my father had given me when I was sixteen and out of fear for my safety threw it into the pond, I saw how deeply this was all affecting him and how he struggled to process his own feelings.

I had mistaken his stoicism for dismissal, when in fact he was just as confused as I was. I felt like damaged goods, and like I forced David into something he didn't ask for.

When the time came to address our sexual relationship, we were both afraid to say what we felt. Our therapist instinctively recognized this.

"One of the challenges I see with the two of you, as a couple, is that the deep love you have for one another prevents you from saying what you really feel, and those things need to be brought out into the open."

Looking at both of us, she asked us to trust that we could untangle it with her. Reluctantly we agreed and started in on the harrowing process of releasing an honesty that we never imagined possible.

I could not grasp the complexities of how I felt about sex. When I would set out to reveal something I felt ashamed of, David would respond with, "I get it. That makes sense," which paved the way for deeper truths.

I admitted I still wished I wasn't gay, and that the idea of sex as I once knew it often made me feel sick to my stomach. My words brought me to tears. I was able to explore my judgments about gay sex and the normality of heterosexual sex as I saw it. I longed for a clear sexual identity that I could rely on, but no label seemed to suit me.

David listened, tearing up and telling me it was okay. I could not comprehend the deep level of compassion he was able to show in the depths of what were our darkest moments.

He shared his own issues around sex, and for the first time, I was able to hear him without berating myself for not being enough for him.

The quandary of whether or not we could fulfill each other's sexual ideals was no longer the issue. The question became how to find our way back to an intimacy we knew we were capable of. We now understood that intimacy could mean many things, determined only by us. It was undeniable that we had been through experiences that might derail any couple. With a new appreciation for what we had discovered, we set out to reconnect and challenge ourselves to look at things differently, demanding honesty from one another regardless of fear.

As I tried to maintain balance between my tumultuous personal life and my professional life, I came down with a debilitating case of neurologic Lyme disease. Ignoring brief periods of memory loss, disorientation, and tingling numbness down the side of my body became impossible, and I had to admit something was very wrong.

I was outfitted with a line in my arm in order to receive daily infusions of antibiotic therapy to my heart. It was inconvenient and exhausting, adding another layer of misery to an already challenging time.

When a friend said to me, "God doesn't give us more than we can handle," I wanted to scream, *You have no idea what the fuck you are saying.* My lethargy hadn't hindered the anger that constantly churned in great waves through my body and mind.

As a result of the treatment, I was advised not to drink alcohol. Having to go for routine liver checks during the course of infusions kept me sober for an agonizing twenty-eight days. Vacillating between periods of nausea, headaches, and weakness, I told myself this was a sign to slow down and curtail my drinking. I told myself this was a wake-up call to focus more on my health, especially now that I had made the decision, at least as of that day, not to kill myself. If I intended to go on living, I should make an effort to be healthier.

My plan worked for about a week after the tube was removed from my tender arm. I had lost weight during the treatment and felt grateful to have a less-swollen face. I started on my regimen of one martini in the evening, vowing not to have any more after that. David embraced the change and had no trouble adhering to the new rules. But in what seemed like lightning speed, I was back with a vengeance, having multiple cocktails followed by a bottle of wine. David and I had always been drinking buddies, a shared ritual that I believed helped us to connect. Now, I was outpacing him as he looked on more critically.

Chapter Fifteen

After a few years, my parents could no longer afford to stay in the house. The plan, which I learned about from my sister, was that they would move in with her, into an in-law apartment that was yet to be built. I was angry she was taking them in and urged her to consider alternatives.

"There are no alternatives. The apartments they can afford are depressing, and Dad said he'd rather die than move into one of them. I have no choice."

I told her she was making a grievous mistake. My heart ached at the thought of my father living under the same roof as my niece. The idea that my sister would take in my unpredictable mother made me sick to my stomach. Not being able to say what was really on my mind preyed on my anxiety.

"I have to ask you something," she said.

Palms sweating chest tight, I stayed silent.

"Did Dad do something sexual to you?"

I felt exposed and put on the spot. Shame consumed me, and I stumbled over my answer.

"No. I'm not sure."

She remained silent.

We had arrived at the truth, but I wasn't prepared to face it. I wished she hadn't asked me.

I felt like a coward. I was no longer a child, yet I still felt the threat of my parents, their control and manipulations breathing down my neck.

Eileen and I held onto so many secrets, some together and some that were ours alone to bear. I thought if I said yes now, I would fall apart trying to face this nightmare.

I ended our conversation abruptly, with an excuse that I had another call. The distance that followed us after that day grew, but I welcomed it because I was forced to come to terms with something that seemed incomprehensible.

The memory of having been penetrated by my father ran through my bloodstream; it poisoned me.

I was running out of effective ways to numb the truth as the flashbacks became clearer, my body memory informing me more aggressively that what I feared was indeed real. I was sick to my stomach as I recalled him forcing himself into my mouth when I was a young boy, still in my Winnie the Pooh pajamas. The image of him naked and towering over me stalked my thoughts, making me feel vulnerable and under attack despite the fact that I was now a grown man in his late thirties. The thought of him putting me to bed incited stifling terror as I recalled how my face felt in the pillow, and the excruciating pain that followed.

I skirted the issue with my therapist for many sessions over the course of months, incapable of saying all that was pummeling my memory.

I did not want to believe that a grown man could enter the body of a young child, and that the grown man had been my own father, and that young child me.

Finding the courage to merely allude to the fact that those things happened was hard enough.

I did not want to hear my therapist's compassion, or ascertain that she already had her suspicions. Instead, I said only enough to allow it into the room, to float in between us for a discussion at some other date.

But my plan failed.

I finally left her office one day carrying the burden of the truth that struggled to work its way out of my system, instead of consuming me. It was too much. Alone back at the shop after that session, I went into the bathroom.

I stared in the mirror as the tears released themselves and I shook my head *no*. I succumbed to the salty bile that rose in my mouth and threw up, now sobbing on the floor. I remained there for a long time, unable to stop the heaving that wracked my body and made my head pound. *No. No, no, no.*

The reality was too much to face, as I pictured my small body being penetrated and violated, setting the course for the painful years that followed.

That night, I could not reveal to David what had happened. Instead, I quickly drank myself into a stupor while he watched with concern and frustration. He often noticed the change in my speech pattern that indicated that I was not stable, and I worked hard to watch for the signs that I was slurring. That night I couldn't disguise the downward spiral I was falling into.

I went upstairs and took Klonopin, losing track of how many I had slipped under my tongue, wanting the numbing effect to take over. David found me crouched on the bathroom floor, empty wrappers from the dissolvable tablets in my hand. He demanded to know how many I had taken.

"Three, I think."

"Then where are the other wrappers? What have you done?" He asked in exasperation.

Confused and disoriented, I just stared at the floor as he left the room. He returned with the phone and sternly told me to speak to my therapist, who was on the other line. She and David decided it best that I go to the emergency room. I was angry and embarrassed and insisted to the doctor it was all an innocent mistake. My blood alcohol content was very high, which gave her cause for alarm. Realizing I was possibly facing a lecture or suggestion of some form of treatment, I turned the situation around, charming the doctor until she was convinced I was not some lunatic off the street. I swore I was in good hands with David, and that I would curtail my drinking.

What I couldn't change was David's searing stare, knowing I was manipulating things. He was angry with me and with my therapist, thinking she had missed the signs that I was unstable.

But I knew the truth of what unfolded. Not only was I coming to terms with having been sodomized, but also I had not been honest, even with my therapist. I knew I was at a crossroads, and had to either divulge what was plaguing me or work even harder to bury it and find new ways to pretend it never happened.

I walked around in a daze for weeks after that night. It felt as though I was hovering outside of my body, watching myself go through the motions of each day in a trance.

While out shopping for supplies, I wandered into the sporting goods section. I knew what I needed and felt the cool handle of the aluminum bat under my fingertips as I moved it. I made my choice quickly and assertively, holding it firmly in my hand. I tucked it into the back seat and smiled as I looked in the rearview mirror, knowing I was now prepared.

I was consumed with fantasies of killing my father. I'd lose myself in thoughts of arriving back in Levittown, showing up at my sister's house, and beating his car with the bat until he emerged from the house. My hands would clench as I thought of striking the sideview mirrors and hearing the crackling sound of the glass as it shattered from the windows. Once he appeared in front of me, I'd ask only one question, "Why?" Sure to hear one of his standard pathetic responses of "I just wanted you to love me," or "Anything I did was never meant to hurt you," I'd raise my bat, striking him first in the jaw to shut him up, rendering him unable to speak another delusional lie. Then I'd bring the bat down on his skull again and again until it lacked any recognizable form, the pavement covered with his blood and bone fragments.

My fantasy ended there. I never thought of what would happen afterward. I didn't care to think of any repercussions. But the sense of calm that came over me after those thoughts made it hard to believe there was any downside in carrying them out.

During a particularly productive therapy session, I confided that I had purchased a bat and kept it in the back seat of my car. Not disguising her concern, my therapist asked me more about it. I explained that I felt safer, and should I decide to confront my father face to face, I thought it best to have protection. After all, it was better than carrying a gun. She listened intently, but at the end of our hour, calmly asked that I make a promise to her not to do anything that would get me arrested or land me in jail. She sympathized with my justifiable rage, but made it clear she believed there were other ways for me to work through it.

Our commitment to work with a couple's therapist proved to be beneficial. The energy between us softened, and David and I were surprised at our increasing lightheartedness. As laughter made its grand reentry, we shared more about the ups and downs of our days, as well as the dynamics of our families, and we spoke more frequently about the bond that we knew was still there.

For the first time, we spoke of flirtations and encounters with other men, and I felt less ashamed speaking of my own methods as I continued to figure out what my sexual identity consisted of. The level of honesty we explored would often bring me to tears, because what I had previously perceived as shameful was met with understanding and acceptance.

David admitted he could not possibly comprehend all I had been through. He wanted me to feel assured that he was committed to our relationship, and that together we would tackle whatever we had to.

I heard his words, but I had a hard time believing that after he knew the truth, he'd still love me. I had acted out so harshly against him, wishing he would leave my life in some way, craving the easy way out. Now with his display of determination, I was faced with confronting the whole truth and living up to my promise of no more secrets.

I told him.

I saw his face express anger, sadness, and sympathy as I spoke of all that my father had done. He held me as I sobbed, and I was stunned to be able to embrace the comfort he provided.

My biggest fear was that after having heard what had been done to me, David would reject me. His willingness proved otherwise, opening up opportunities for us to grow and heal together. He was a miracle.

I remained committed to finding distractions and planned on throwing a large dinner for clients. It remained a good way to soothe my frenetic brain, and I was able to avoid revealing what was going on behind the scenes. David and I relished in the escapism of these elaborate evenings. The evening played out beautifully—the table, flowers, trays of cocktails, linens, music—all was in order, and we celebrated in the warmth of the triumph. I had fully embraced the ways of Camille and took great pride in bringing them to life. For David and me.

As things wound down and we were left alone, we talked in front of the fire. Interrupting his own train of thought, he looked at me and asked, "Are you okay?"

I was not. Anger stirred in me, but I could not pinpoint where it was coming from. "I'm not sure. Honestly, I feel like throwing this tray of glasses across the room."

"Do what you need to do."

I grabbed the tray of glasses—some empty, some with liquid remnants of the evening's inebriation—and walked into the kitchen. I paused, looking across the room, gripped the tray firmly in two hands, and turned as I forcefully let it fly and crash into the cabinets, sending glass into the air. I stood there staring, my face red and pounding from rage, as I grabbed empty wine bottles and hurled them against the same target. David came up behind, and I could feel him near me.

"Don't come near me." I warned.

"Okay. Can I do anything?" His voice was trembling.

"No. I'm going outside." My voice was steady and determined.

I went to my car, slamming the door after I retrieved my weapon. The cold air caught me off guard, and I felt the icy sting of it against my sweaty face. Without thinking twice, I turned and faced the field as I clutched the bat firmly in my hand. The moon lit up the space around me, its reflection bouncing off the shiny galvanized garbage cans over my shoulder. Two cans sat side by side, their lids clamped tight in an attempt to discourage the raccoons and bears. I lifted the bat high over my head and brought it down onto the lid of one of the cans, sending the crashing sound of metal on metal echoing down the road and across the pond. The image of my father burned like a villain behind my eyelids, and with every downward thrust I saw myself smashing his face, tearing at his skin and crushing his skull. I could not repeat the motion fast enough, my arms vibrating with each impact. The groans that came from deep inside of my stomach increased until they became guttural screams, burning my throat, and leaving the taste of blood in my mouth. That fueled me even more, and I relentlessly slammed the bat down, sending trash flying about my head and pieces of metal from the lid and handles ricocheting off the stone walls. As I stared at the flattened wreckage, the emotion that had threatened to emerge for so long finally gave way, causing me to fall to my knees in sobs, lying across the frozen ground pulling my knees in tight.

I finally stood, leaving my bat next to the crumpled garbage bins, and went inside. David sat waiting for me and hung up the phone abruptly. I walked silently upstairs, and he helped me into bed, kissing me on the forehead and pulling the covers up around me, a moment of kindness that soothed my anxious mind and aching body.

We said little to one another the next morning. My hands were blistered and bloodied, still pulsing from repeated blunt force impact. The muscles in my back sent spasms down my legs and my throat was raw, causing me to clear it every few seconds. David asked me how I was doing, and I smiled.

"Much better. I don't know what happened."

"That needed to come out. I'm really proud of you."

I looked at him and saw tears in his eyes, and not being able to contain my own any longer, I released them in a stream down my face and onto my shirt. David and I held each other, offering comfort for both my pain and his fear for what he had witnessed.

When I had ventured out with my bat, David became concerned for my safety, wondering if I was experiencing some sort of breakdown. He called my therapist and explained to her what was unfolding on the other side of the living room window. She could hear what was transpiring and reassured him it was okay, and that if he could, he should allow me to continue uninterrupted. Seeing me that way terrified him, and in a show of solidarity, my therapist remained on the phone with him, listening and soothing his state of mind with her incredible compassion and knowledge, until I returned to him safely.

I could not comprehend the rage I had been holding onto and how violently it had emerged. What was most troublesome was that it all felt so natural, and the mere idea of taking my father's life put me at ease. I was not relieved that I had not acted on it; rather I felt I had agreed to a settlement. By allowing myself that fantasy, I began to understand the depths of anger, sadness, and shame that I had held onto since I was a very young child.

In the aftermath, I uncovered my raw feelings and searched for a way to not let them rule my life forever.

———

I cancelled countless visits from my sister and niece.

My well-intended plans created a feeling of such vulnerability that the idea of seeing them was unbearable. The disappointment in my niece's voice was enough to bring me to tears, and Eileen's growing frustration dismayed me.

I reluctantly decided it was time to be honest with her. I kept things short and to the point, confessing that yes, my father had sexually abused me. I went on to say that I was worried about him being close to my niece.

Eileen's rage disarmed me.

"You lied to me, Larry J. You lied."

My apologies and excuses of not being ready to talk about the truth fell on deaf ears. Her own anger poured through the receiver straight to my heart. I felt responsible now that Eileen had taken my parents in, despite her belief she had no choice. Nothing I said could change her lifelong guilt and sense of responsibility.

The feeling that I was alone often overwhelmed me. While David was supportive, he could not possibly know the feelings and demons I lived with. I wondered how other men who had experienced such things managed their own lives. My therapist reassured me that I wasn't crazy to feel the way I did, but I longed to speak to other men who could relate to how I felt.

An online search resulted in me discovering an organization that provided support for male victims of sexual abuse. I felt apprehensive clicking on the link, feeling as though I'd be found out in some way. I stealthily created a login name and password, gaining access to the online support channels.

I carefully watched the dialogue that transpired between the men who showed up in the various discussion groups. What surprised me most was how normal they sounded. For the most part, I witnessed a respectful dialogue of experiences and ways to handle triggers. I was intrigued and explored the site further, discovering weekend workshops at various times and places were offered throughout the year.

My therapist had not heard of the organization and was cautious, looking into it further before giving her blessing. The protection I felt from her soothed my nerves and offered me a form of safety I had come to trust. David deferred to my judgment, showing me he would support any endeavor I believed would help. The next workshop was just a few weeks away. Putting my fears aside, I registered.

David and I made an agreement to not speak while I was away at the retreat. I believed that in order to fully commit to the process, I needed to avoid any distractions from my life back at home. This would be the first time in the history of our relationship we would not be in daily contact. Even in our worst periods, we connected consistently in some way. I understood from the intake interview over the phone, no alcohol or drugs were allowed. I worried about not being able to drink when inevitable feelings were stirred up. The phone interview was difficult, with me having to answer personal questions about my perpetrator, my therapist, the supportive person in my life, and my drinking and drug use. I steadied myself after giving each answer.

When the therapist interviewing me said, "This next question is a difficult one, but one we feel is critical before allowing you to attend a weekend. Have you ever been arrested for sexual abuse or have you had tendencies to abuse others?"

My heart sank. I understood the question and its importance, but it underlined the gravity of sexual abuse. I answered clearly. No.

I arrived in Montreal the night before I was due. The small retreat center was about an hour's drive away from the airport hotel where I settled in for a few drinks, knowing they'd be my last for the next few days. I was terrified and started to second-guess my decision, wondering if anyone would possibly be able to understand my angry and emotional mind.

The retreat center was nestled alongside a small lake, a serene setting for what was sure to be anything but. I found my way to the registration desk, mortified to find men walking around with nametags, hating that my anonymity would be broken. I felt ashamed knowing that the name I'd inscribe in magic marker and wear across my chest was the same name my father had. I suddenly wished I had followed through on my fantasy of legally changing it. I was handed a welcome package with an itinerary, forms to fill out, a water bottle, and a journal with instructions to meet in the main assembly space in an hour.

I found my room and paced, looking out to the lake, grateful I had decided to spend the extra money to have my own room. The next hour ticked away slowly, causing me to nervously look at my watch every few minutes. I was out of my element and I felt it. Here, no one knew my business or me. The life I worked so hard to make look perfect and elegant didn't matter here. I was afraid they wouldn't like me, or worse yet, not believe me.

As I made my way to the appointed room, I forced a smile, passing the other men. I watched and analyzed their movements. I walked in on a large circle of chairs, the seats filling up as the others found their way. I sat next to a man who gave me a smile, his boyish face betraying the sadness in his eyes. I wondered what his story was.

"Hi, I'm Ron," he offered with a grin.

I introduced myself, and he asked if this was my first weekend.

"Yes, it is. I'm a little nervous. How about you?"

"It's my sixth."

Noticing the surprised look on my face, he explained that as he continued his own healing, he found that going to the weekends offered him support at each new juncture. The fact that he was a regular put me at ease, even as I shuddered seeing boxes of tissues placed throughout the circle. I wondered how long it would take for me to fall apart.

My eyes scanned the room as the circle filled in. There were about twenty-seven of us along with eight therapists. The men spanned generations: the youngest not yet twenty-one, and the eldest well into his seventies. Some were extremely thin while others obese. I looked for signs that other gay men were in attendance, but it was hard to tell because an androgynous quality seemed to possess the majority. One man sat close to a supporting column in the middle of the room, his right arm draped around it as if for protection. It pained me to look at him; his expression gave away so much anguish and vulnerability. I couldn't avert my eyes though. I felt drawn into his darkness and related to him in a way I did not yet understand. I envied him that seat and the support of that column. I felt shaky and wished I too had something to lean on for stability.

The therapists walked us through the itinerary, emphasizing how honored they were that we took the courageous step to attend what was certain to be an intimidating but rewarding experience. They covered safety exercises and ground rules, reiterating no sexual contact, no discrimination, no controlled substances or alcohol, and respect for one another's boundaries. As the afternoon unfolded, we were broken down into smaller groups with each group assigned two therapists. In our smaller assemblies, we would share our stories with the understanding that we, as individual men, could indeed heal. The therapists in my small group were warm and nurturing without being cloying. I was relieved to be in a group with a female therapist. It was what I was used to, and I embraced the feminine energy.

There was tremendous buildup to the sharing of our stories. My stomach soured as the hour drew near, and I hoped I would not get sick, knowing it was one of the ways I responded to memories.

I had never told anyone my whole story, from start to finish.

The idea of having time to speak, with six men listening, made me want to hide.

I was relieved to not have to go first, but that meant I started to listen. What I heard was horrifying, gut wrenching, confusing, and bewildering. I heard men who also had been sexually abused by their father saying things I thought only I felt. Other men had been victimized by their mothers, teachers, coaches, clergy, and in one case, a pediatrician.

I struggled to wrap my head around the similarities of the resulting shame, isolation, self-loathing, and ways in which we all attempted to cope. I felt angry that we shared those traits. My heart went out to the men who believed their experience was consensual even though they, like me, were not yet of kindergarten age when it happened. Many of them had also been abused more than once and by more than one perpetrator.

As I absorbed their words, I cried along with them, where those tears originated. I could feel my jaw tighten as the sharing circled to me. The group took a collective breath after each story was shared, a breath I found hard to capture.

I started my story by saying the most difficult part—that my perpetrator was my father. I could feel the lump in my throat tighten as I spoke of his smothering love, ways he showed me affection, and how feeling his erection pressed against me was a regular occurrence. I detailed my memories of being forced to perform oral sex on him and the difficulty I had in accepting that he had sodomized me at such a young age.

I posed the questions that still taunted my thoughts: When had it stopped? How was it possible to sodomize such a young body? Did my mother know? I spoke of what happened with Robert and the repulsion that ensued as a result of knowing that those acts had already been done to me. I talked about the hunting trips and the guilt I felt for depriving my father of his precious father-son time, and I admitted that I struggled as an adult to understand my own sexuality.

When I finished, the therapists instructed me to go around our circle making eye contact with each and every man for a moment before moving on to the next, a grounding exercise to help bring us back to the present. As I looked to my left and my eyes met the man sitting next to me, I saw his tears for the first time. He had been crying as I shared my story. Now, looking at him, I slowly broke down into sobs, then attempted to look at the other men in the circle.

We had things in common that I wished we didn't, unspoken things we understood about one another.

The weekend progressed with more ways to connect, process, and heal. I felt fortunate I had a therapist to go back to, and felt disheartened so many of my fellow participants were returning to their lives without support in place. For many of them, this was their first foray into coming to terms with what had happened to them. In the evenings, when we had time to socialize, we shared our stories of how we had acted out. Alcohol and other drugs were common tools among us, and for many, acting out sexually was the norm. The majority of men I met also struggled with their sexual identity, and in some cases, struggled with their gender. I wasn't convinced I would ever learn how to be a sexual being without triggers, flashbacks, and confusion.

Over time, I did believe that if I worked hard, I could find a way to live a life where my past did not consume me. For me, that meant continued dedication to therapy and putting into practice what David and I had learned was necessary for our relationship to survive. Honesty, trust, and willingness to communicate were essential, despite how uncomfortable it could be.

Maintaining better boundaries with clients and friends remained a challenge, as I was easily pulled back into what I felt I "should" be doing.

Eileen and I struggled with our relationship, and I felt the gravity of the situation anytime we tried to speak. I wondered if my father was in the room whenever she asked to call me back. The idea that they were all essentially under one roof again made me cringe. Discussing Eileen consumed a lot of my time in therapy as I evaluated whether or not I should cut ties with her, at least temporarily. My niece was getting older, and I started to see the potential in a relationship with her outside of my sister.

My therapist suggested that I could ask Eileen to come in for a session. Eileen welcomed the suggestion. She admitted she was nervous, but agreed, saying she would do anything to help me.

Eileen chose to sit next to me on the therapist's couch that I had claimed as my own for more than five years—my sister, who had nurtured me more than my own mother ever had and had been my biggest ally for as long as I could remember. It broke my heart that we had suffered a fracture and were now trying to find a way back to that place of trust that had at one time defined us.

Eileen stated that while she did not recall anything our father had done to me, she was there to show her support.

When my therapist referred to us having had such a damaging and violent childhood, Eileen sat up, going rigid as she said, "I am not prepared to discuss anything that happened with my mother."

Her energy shifted, and my instinct was to take her in my arms, hold her, and tell her it was okay. It became clear in that moment there were things I did not know. I felt angry and disgusted but simultaneously closer to my big sister. I confessed I had been struggling to come to terms with the truth for years, and that I had regretted lying to her about the abuse.

Hearing that she forgave me helped me to understand that we might be able to find a way to heal many of the wounds that we shared, both of us committed to the well-being and safety of my niece. I had not anticipated her willingness, and while I remained conflicted, I could not deny the deep love I had for her.

Chapter Sixteen

Finding peace with what my father had done eluded me. In my efforts to gain acceptance, I replayed the stories of his childhood over and over again in my head as I searched for some thread of understanding. I separated the facts from my suspicions. I thought of my two great uncles who grew up in the house along with him. They had been unusually close, sharing not only a bedroom but also a bed, until they died just a few months apart in their seventies. I only had vague memories of them, but now it struck me as odd that in that big house they had chosen that arrangement. My father never elaborated much on them, aside from some tales of a sordid past that included drinking and gambling, traits that ran through our family bloodlines.

When it came to sharing what had happened with anyone other than David or my therapist, I proceeded with caution, having experienced mixed results and fears of being judged, or worse, answering questions I wasn't ready for. The subject of family came up frequently in social situations, but I would skirt the issue, revealing as little detail as possible. If pushed, I'd sometimes release a vague comment that my father had been inappropriate to me as a child. I couldn't stomach that word— inappropriate—as it didn't accurately describe my experience, yet it was often easier than the impact of saying, "sexually abused."

An early revelation proved devastating. I shared my experience with Pedro, a man I considered a close friend. He shook his head and offered a hug before handing me a drink and changing the subject. A week or so later, he made a joke that my father had been my first boyfriend, my first male lover. Shocked and embarrassed, I laughed along with him, making light of an experience *he* was clearly uncomfortable with. I felt ashamed for not standing up to him, but I understood more than ever it was a subject most would prefer not to discuss, finding it easier to ignore or dismiss the truth. After that, I was even more cautious in my choice to divulge.

I now had a clear understanding of how silence perpetuates abuse.

By not talking about it, it's allowed to continue to happen uninterrupted, in plain sight, as my father had mastered. And not many people want to talk about it.

David remained an anchor at my side, supporting my decision to reveal or not. The small cluster of friends who knew my story grew over time, but only after I felt safe. Even then, I was still caught off guard by a response.

On one occasion, I was invited to an extravagant lunch with a client who had become a trusted friend. I had shared the truth with her, and spoke of the struggles I faced in day-to-day life. She listened with a sympathetic ear, offering me a kindness I desperately needed but didn't know how to ask for. Feeling I could rely on her confidence, I discussed triggers, anxiety, and depression. I went on to say that sometimes I felt overwhelming sadness being around children.

The energy shifted quickly, and I saw her shoulders tense as I guessed what was coming. With my hand under the table, I took a firm grip on my leg and squeezed it until it hurt, a technique I used to deflect something uncomfortable that I was about to experience.

Avoiding eye contact, she asked, "Are you finding yourself attracted to kids?" The question stung, and I felt sad but compelled to explain.

"No, thank God. I struggle around kids because I can't imagine someone doing to them what was done to me. It's something I find impossible to understand."

I stared at her, hoping she'd meet my eyes. Instead, looking down at the table she simply said, "I'm sorry I asked that, Larry."

The silence lingered for some time, disrupted only by the waiter refilling our water glasses.

Our lunch conversation led me to question something that haunted me: Was I the only child my father abused?

It was clear to me something had happened to him, whether or not he was able to acknowledge it. I reread his emails, looking for answers, but I only felt disgusted as I read his repeated excuses. I thought of what brought my parents together, allowing that perfect storm to fester. I even attempted to make sense of the idea of the laws of attraction, believing that there are things that draw us to one another that we may never understand.

Eileen and I did not speak on the phone often—once or twice a month at best. When I did receive a call from her, I always prepared for the worst.

On a trip to New York City with David to celebrate my fortieth birthday, I saw I had missed a call from her. When I called her back, I could tell from her voice something had happened.

"Mom had an incident. She's tried to kill herself."

I tried to digest what she had just said, but my heart went heavy, sinking into my stomach. "What happened? Is she alright?"

David came up behind me and put his hands on my shoulders. My sadness quickly turned to anger as I thought of all of the signs leading up to this that my father had clearly missed. I felt guilty as Eileen shared how things had unfolded.

My parents were in Atlantic City on one of their gambling trips. These trips had been a source of contention for years. My mother hoarded her winnings on the penny slots, demanding more money from my father as she went through her hundred-dollar allotment. My mother was incapable of maintaining friendships and had severed ties with just about everyone. Those trips to Atlantic City were my father's chance to show what a likable and friendly guy he was. He loved the social aspect of sitting at a poker table, seizing the opportunity to charm the dealer and chat with his fellow patrons.

On this trip, however, my mother had plans of her own. She insisted my father leave her alone to play a slot machine. She was still prone to getting lost and wandering off, so he told her where he would be sitting so she could easily find him. As he walked away from her, she went into the ladies room and swallowed handfuls of the prescription medications she brought along for that purpose. She had been drinking, never saying no to the free cocktails the waitresses delivered to her slot machine. She was discovered passed out on the floor in a stall, covered in her own vomit. When the security guards arrived, they asked her whom she was there with, and whom they should contact. She told them she was there alone.

Eileen did not believe this was my mother's first attempt to take her life. She spoke of another time she had gotten inexplicably ill, which Eileen now believed was an overdose. The fragility of mental illness infiltrated Eileen's home and the lives of her husband and daughter.

I was torn: I wanted updates on my mother, yet I didn't. The conflict I felt about not wanting to involve myself, versus missing my fragile mom ran deep.

I felt sad for her, but at the same time, couldn't ignore the complete silence she had imparted on me. And I knew stepping back in would produce disastrous results. Hearing Eileen agree helped me keep my balance and focus on moving forward, as she made it clear my mom wanted nothing to do with me. As painful as that was, I felt forced to accept it.

I often wondered how my father was able to do what he did.

I racked my brain as I asked myself where my mother had been, and questioned whether or not she knew what he was doing to me. I thought of how often she drank, often slipping into oblivion. She took long baths, offering my father some "peace and quiet" as he asked me to watch television with him or visited me in my room.

But now, listening to my sister tell me of her suicide attempt, the word that came back to me was *faggot*. I fixated on my mother calling me a disgusting faggot, then whispering to me, "Those words were meant for him, not you." I shuddered to think she caught him engaged with a man, or even worse, witnessed him abusing me or another child.

I asked myself if what she saw, heard, or knew contributed to her own mental unraveling.

When I heard the sadness in Eileen's voice again a few months later, I feared the worst.

"What happened now?" I asked, dreading the response.

"I need to meet with you. There are some things I need to say about you and Dad."

I pulled off to the side of the road, clutching onto the steering wheel as I watched my knuckles turn white. I heard her crying.

"Okay Eileen. Let's talk, but with my therapist. Is that good?"

She agreed without hesitation, adding, "I love you," as she cried harder.

I was unnerved and emotional as I wondered what she'd say.

Once in my therapist's office, Eileen reiterated that she believed me, putting me at ease just enough to remain grounded, ready to hear what else she had to say. She recalled our relationship as kids and my reliance on her, breaking down into sobs as she talked about me begging her not to leave me at home alone. She spoke of a memory, which I also had, of me wanting to join her and her girlfriends for sleepovers. I would cry and plead with her as she walked through the gate in the chain link fence, asking her to please not leave me. It was clear to her I had been afraid to be left with my father.

Looking up at me, she said, "I'm so sorry. I didn't protect you. I left you with him."

I started to sob and had a hard time thinking clearly. It was a painful moment of honesty and acceptance. I was being given the gift of the assurance that I was not crazy: she too knew he had done those things to his son.

Part of me wanted her to tell me that I had been wrong, but she hadn't done that. Ever. Instead, she took away any remnant of hope that my memory of the abuse I suffered had been a horrible mistake.

Chapter Seventeen

David and I started to look at opportunities to get away and reconnect. We headed to Provincetown, Massachusetts, an environment we loved. We had come through tumultuous times that had almost done us in, and now, slowly, we had a new level of honesty and integrity. We were off to a great start, enjoying dinners, walking along the beach, and settling into our old pastimes of drinking martinis and talking. It felt like we were back to the beginning, but with a refreshed perspective of one another.

We went into one of the local bars for a drink after a long romantic dinner. We were only there a few minutes when I felt my chest tighten. It had been a long time since I had a panic attack, but the sensation was undeniable. I was caught off guard, which only increased the surge of anxiety that quickly became impossible to tame. David went to the bar to fetch our drinks, and by the time he came back I had started to tremble.

"I think I need to leave."

"You okay? Want me to take you back?" he asked with concern.

"I'm fine. You stay. I just need to get out of here."

"Are you sure you're alright?" He looked me in the eye as he spoke. He meant it.

"I'm good; I promise. See you back at the hotel."

I gave him a kiss and headed through the crowd to the door. The air that met my face was fresh and damp, reassuring me I had made the right decision to leave. It took me a few steps to gain my footing and feel stable. I kept my hands in tight fists, feeling the tension rise into my forearms. Slowly, I came into awareness as I tried to comprehend what had happened.

The smell in the bar of stale booze, sweat, and men smothered me and brought back intense memories of my father lying on top of me, the weight of him as he crushed my small form. I froze, just as I had as a young boy when he penetrated me, and I endured mind-numbing pain. I had become detached from the forty-year-old man on vacation, brought back to my father's odor trapped in the smells of that bar.

I took deep breaths as I walked back to the hotel, trying to remind myself that I was okay. I felt threatened by passersby and looked back over my shoulder to make sure I wasn't being followed. I tried to focus on the breeze and the movement of my feet on the pavement, taking comfort in the repetition of my scuffling shoes. By the time I reached the lobby, I had come back into myself. I was exhausted and angry, reaching for an Ativan as soon as I got inside.

By the next day, I was determined to find a solution, to prevent this from happening again. I was angry; I had believed I was making progress only to have a setback. My stubbornness flew into overdrive, and I hashed out ways to combat those situations. I wanted an easy answer and resigned myself to what I knew best.

Clearly I had not had enough to drink that night, and if I were going to stave off future occurrences, I needed to up my game. I felt the enticement of my medicine, booze, more than ever. Having no reason to question what I believed to be medicinal and necessary drinking, my cravings for the numbing effects increased, and I welcomed them.

At first, I was able to slip into my newly dedicated drinking binges without raising an eyebrow. I had mastered the art of deception when it came to hiding my vulnerabilities, taking advantage of the new pact of honesty between David and me. I used it to my benefit, knowing he would not suspect I was indulging as deeply as I was. On trips to the liquor store, I blithely stacked bottles of bourbon, gin, and vodka in my cart, looking at the multiple quantities of each, feeling the weight of necessity.

"Having a party?" the checkout clerk inquired.

"Of course!"

I looked away, not wanting to give up the lie I was telling. I felt contempt for the clerk and couldn't wait to pay the hefty bill and leave. I felt found out, feeling angry as I thought about telling him it was none of his business how I stocked my bar. The voice inside my head turned judgmental as I imagined *his* paltry liquor selection at home, plastic cups stacked in rows nearby. I was a fancy drinker, someone who understood the importance of entertaining in a certain style. Who was this guy anyway? Refusing his help with my boxes, I made two trips as I loaded things into my car, and reminded myself to alter the rotation of stores I frequented, allowing more time to pass before returning to that one.

If David was home, I left my stash in the car, waiting to bring it in and disperse it appropriately once alone. I had cleared a shelf in the basement behind the boxed glassware we used for large parties, referring to it as "back stock." I kept an inventory of our booze on my phone, feeling a rush of urgency as it dwindled down to one bottle of any particular type. I enjoyed Scotch, neat, and used vodka for shots. But gin had become my best friend. What had started off as the most beautiful, perfect gin martini had transformed into a necessary elixir, straight out of the bottle and into a juice glass. It was warm, powerful, and sublime. This type of indulgence became my secret, a private ceremony in which I was the only invitee. I cherished those moments alone in the basement as I retrieved my exquisitely etched glass from its secret hiding place, filling it to the top with Hendrick's or Plymouth.

On most evenings, David joined me in the kitchen, and I pulled the vodka from the freezer drawer, pouring us each a healthy dose. We'd toast, make eye contact, give each other a kiss, and down the contents. He'd place his glass in the sink, and I'd wait, staring out the window over the kitchen sink until I heard the creak of the stairs. I'd refill my glass, keeping it alongside the drain board for easy access, finishing it in quick gulps as I prepared dinner. I'd wash the glass before fixing two martinis, calling him down to join me. On the nights he declined to drink, I became angry and refused to take the night off, but tried to limit the consumption he would witness. I resorted to sneaking shots when he wasn't looking. By the time we sat down, either alone or with guests at our table, I had slipped out of awareness. I dwelled in a divine altered state that kept me at a distance, half engaged and half enveloped in my own thoughts and fantasies. I honored the fact that I was no longer consumed by sadness and thoughts of suicide, drinking more to celebrate all I'd overcome.

"Lar, I'm not sure what happened last night, but your martini really hit you."

David said this, time and time again, the frustration in his voice increasing. Avoiding his eyes, I thought of the extra shots I took and my frequent trips down to the basement during a dinner party to "get more wine," visiting with the stashed bottle of gin as my guests socialized just above me. *If you only knew what I was doing down there.*

My excuses fluctuated from not having had enough to eat to being over tired or overworked, to just having an off night. I would not reveal I had found a new solace in what I believed was inspired drinking.

I was being deceitful, caught up in self-loathing, unable to break away.

My hangovers were sinister, but I refused to let on when I was suffering. I'd leap out of bed as if I was fine, steadying myself in the bathroom and trying not to throw up. I believed Ativan was the answer to my insomnia, and never ended an evening without one or two before bed. Klonopin was my standby, and I'd resort to those more often during the day to ease my trembling hands. Driving the fifteen minutes to my store each day was agony. I'd lower the window in the winter and let the frigid breeze numb my skin. In the summer, the stifling heat nauseated me, and I'd have to chill the car before I got into it for fear of being sick.

I did what I knew best and threw more elaborate dinner parties. It was a perfect way for me to justify my indulgence, and with other people in the room, David was sure to be distracted.

I planned a grand Moroccan feast for a large group of friends. I carefully plotted my menu, opting to make a multitude of dishes with an endless supply of drinks, just as Camille had inspired me to do. David and I had a reputation for pouring substantial cocktails, and I laughed when someone commented on our eight-ounce martini glasses, saying they were of modest size. By the time everyone was seated, I was in a complete blackout.

The next morning it was clear David was not speaking to me. As I said good morning, he remained silent.

"Do you have anything to say?" he inquired angrily.

"About what?"

He stared back at me. "You don't remember, do you?"

I didn't remember anything. I felt bad; clearly I had been unkind, and I racked my brain to remember if I had justifiable cause. I was at a loss, having no idea what had transpired.

When I saw the remnants of our party, I felt ashamed. The table was a mess—spilled drinks and broken glasses, candle wax across the table, leftover food sitting out as the cats grazed the remains. I stammered as I made promises to watch how much I drank from then on. I apologized for my altered speech when I was drunk and his inevitable concern for my safety. That concern brought back the times I fantasized about killing myself, and the dark places I retreated to. I believed I had moved past those horrible times, but couldn't grasp why I continued to rely on alcohol.

I dodged any conversations regarding my intoxication with my therapist, but it was unavoidable when I appeared at sessions bloated, hungover, and at times smelling of alcohol. I remained convinced I was not an alcoholic, and that if I wanted to, I could control or slow down my drinking. I was not my mother, and I was adamant I could prove it, by drinking like a gentleman. I would defy the definitions of alcoholism and prove I was above that.

Rebuilding trust with David, I had resumed trips into New York City. Heading in to meet with a new client, I checked into my hotel, and without thinking twice, walked up Broadway to a liquor store. I wandered the aisles, grabbing a bottle of Bombay and Ketel One—enough for my two-night stay, assuming I'd make it out to a bar or two to supplement. I downed a few shots before heading out to dinner. The chilly February evening beckoned me, and I was ready to indulge in an evening alone. I headed to the closest restaurant I could find, and before removing my coat, ordered a gin martini, up. I loved dining alone. I would scan the room, lost in my thoughts, organizing the jumble of ideas and concerns that were ever present.

I ate well, enjoying a second martini and a glass of wine. When I got back to my hotel, I fell into a deep sleep after taking a second Ativan, relieved to be anonymous and alone in the city. When I woke, I could not lift my head. I lay there slowly coming into the awareness that I felt weighted down. My head pounded, and as I opened one eye, the room twirled in somersaults around me. It took me a while to remember where I was, and I tried to replay the evening over in my head. I wondered if I was missing a critical event that would have created the feeling of having been hit by a truck. I thought of my dinner, asking myself if I had come down with food poisoning or if perhaps someone had slipped something into my drink. I had not had any more than usual—if anything, it was a lighter night than I normally indulged in. I found the clock, realizing I had just a half an hour to get downtown to meet my client.

I shook all over, and couldn't bear to get in the shower. As I leaned over to splash water on my face, I fought the urge to throw up, fearing I wouldn't stop. I moved like an invalid—careful, planned, and pained— not being able to fathom what had gone wrong. I instructed the cab driver to head downtown and opened my window, seeking the familiar sensation of the cold on my face. I supported my head in my hands, asking the driver to stop as my stomach gurgled, and the taste of bile rose in my throat. Out on the street I found the nearest trash bin and leaned on it, not caring enough to worry about who might see me. I wished I could throw up, to purge myself of the violent poison I was convinced was inside me.

I stumbled into a cafe and ordered a coffee, but the smell sickened me and I threw it out. I made my way down the few blocks to the shop where I was to meet my client. I wandered around the first floor, praying I did not smell of alcohol, and that she wouldn't notice I was wobbly. I struggled to maintain my focus as we examined piles of antique carpets, and I feigned patience as she complained about the prices, asking for discounts. I hated her and I wanted our shopping spree over with. Turning to leave, she asked if I was okay.

"Yes, I'm fine. Just a little run down."

I was grateful to have not made any other appointments, eager to return to my room.

I lamented that it was Tuesday, one of my two weekly therapy days. I did not want to speak to my therapist and contemplated cancelling our phone session at the last minute, knowing full well that she would not accept that without questioning me. Lying on the bed staring at the ceiling, I reluctantly dialed her number.

"Hello, dear Larry."

I told her more than I had anticipated. I suddenly needed to fight the denial I believed had been my ally.

"I think I have a problem." The words floated around the room, mocking me and telling me I was a loser. She listened with compassion and reassured me I would be okay. After our session, I remained motionless on the bed for hours as I contemplated what to do next.

On my second night, I had plans to see an old friend for dinner. Nicholas had worked at my shop a few years earlier and left to move to the city to pursue his own creative career. When he was my employee, I forgave his shortcomings. I chalked up his consistent lateness and falling asleep at his desk as a product of his youth. I had not known that he was indulging in drugs and alcohol to the extent that he was. Once he moved to the city, his downward spiral consumed him, and after a brush with death, he found his way to sobriety.

Nicholas had tolerated my visits on many occasions. I'd arrive in the city wanting to spoil him with extravagant dinners while I drank to oblivion, making advances and pushing the limits of his tolerance. Still, he never abandoned me, allowing our strong connection to grow despite my inebriation.

As I walked in, he was already seated, his back toward me. Thirteen years my junior and strikingly handsome, I usually beamed in his presence but found myself now dreading eye contact. He stood to hug me, reminding me of our deep, inexplicable connection.

I sat down, and he started the conversation off in his usual way. "How's my Larry doing?"

I had been looking over his shoulder, focusing on the people walking through the door. I heard him but hesitated, knowing this was my opportunity to be honest.

"I'm not so good." Tears filled my eyes, but he just stared at me, smiling in his reassuring way. "I think I have a problem."

Nicholas reached out, taking my trembling hands in his, his eyes never leaving mine. "Can you do something for me?"

I had never heard him ask for anything, ever, and looked up to meet his gaze. "Yes, of course."

"Don't have a drink tonight. Can you do that?"

Unable to speak, I simply nodded.

Admitting I was an alcoholic filled me with shame, and as far as I was concerned, it reflected my true weakness. I could not comprehend how to manage my life and my feelings without the ability to numb.

I also couldn't ignore the facts: my trembling hands, swollen appearance, and the cravings that struck by three o'clock every afternoon.

I asked myself how I could continue to lie to David and myself. I survived years of suicidal thinking, and now I was slowly killing myself anyway. I imagined my father laughing at me, telling me, "See, you are just like your mother. You are Karen. I was right all along."

Evenings were the most difficult. I did not know what I was going to do with the long stretches of time I used to spend drinking. I was angry and emotional as my moods fluctuated, and I worked hard to stay away from a drink, delving into a program that helped me to maintain my day-to-day sobriety.

With David's support, I waded through the guilt I felt about abandoning him as a drinking buddy, worried he wouldn't find me fun anymore. It was difficult to confess to him the depths I had sunk to. The hiding place in the basement, the extra shots, and gin by the glassful while his back was turned. He listened while I spoke of the lies, embracing me with compassion.

What I had not anticipated was the necessity of looking at all of the areas of my life where my addictive behavior had manifested.

At times I felt cheated, wondering how I would soothe my nerves and indulge my melancholy episodes. I had given up the use of Klonopin and Ativan the same day I had my last drink, knowing that my use of those prescriptions had crossed a line. I handed over any leftover pills to David and he made them disappear. I turned to eating more sugar and obsessively looking at my phone to pass the endless hours of restlessness.

For the year that followed, I tried to lose myself in any activity that would help me escape my own thoughts. Now, I only had myself to answer to, backed up against a wall when it came to my sexual behavior and obsessiveness in trying to figure out things.

Chapter Eighteen

Stacks of antique plates were piled up on the counter next to the kitchen sink, waiting to be washed. That sight used to be daunting; my head would pound and I'd feel dizzy after a night of blackout drinking. Those mornings filled me with enormous shame. I'd witness the wreckage and force myself to work quickly to minimize the mess before David awoke, my hands trembling and waves of nausea coming over me.

But now I reflected on how nice the evening had been, and took a minute to notice my clarity. I actually remembered the conversations I'd had with friends. When I promised to do something for someone in the past, the request was often lost in the turmoil of my drunkenness. Now I found I was able to keep my promises. I did not take those moments for granted. I knew full well that for me, staying away from a drink required effort. But now, taking the morning off from my usual manic rush to the store was one of the rewards sobriety provided, and with a clear head, I set out to tackle a new day.

Chuck arrived to take his girlfriend's young son fishing in our pond. David and I knew him well, a local handyman who had done work on our house over the years. I watched as he helped the four-year-old out of the pickup truck and was struck by the sweetness of them together, fishing poles in hand.

I often looked at situations like those with alarm, not feeling as though I had a perspective on what was normal. Often when I heard stories of parents comforting their children in bedrooms at night, I couldn't help but cringe, my own experience reminding me of what the other side of those visits could look like. It was uncomfortable to always try to judge a situation as safe or not. My brain often felt like a pinball machine as my memories of doing things with my dad became intertwined with the present day.

I returned to my task at hand, trying to calm the fluttering that started in my chest as my thoughts rambled. I caught glimpses of my visiting fishermen, hooking worms and casting out their lines across the narrow body of water as the red and white bobbers bounced around on the surface. I fell back into thoughts of fishing with my dad, pushing myself to recall the peace I felt being out along the banks of a stream as I learned to fly fish. I was deliberate in my efforts to try to hang onto whatever good memories I could. But in an instant my thoughts betrayed me, turning to the television fishing programs my dad used to make me watch with him on Saturday afternoons. The father-son time that became something it never should have been.

I turned my focus on the hot, sudsy dishwater; the music; and the movement of my hands, choosing whatever I had available to shake my recollections. A glare caught my eye as I looked up, and I strained to see where they had gone. Squinting, I looked around the perimeter of the pond, not seeing any trace of Chuck and the boy. I started to busy myself with worry as I wondered where they had gone. I walked to the living room, its windows with a broader view, but still nothing. Panic took over, my chest tightened, and I became terrified for that little boy.

I heard David's footsteps on the floor above my head, and as he walked downstairs, he asked casually, "How's the clean up?"

But I didn't respond. I stood staring out the window, praying they would call my bluff and walk out into view.

David approached me and put his hand on my shoulder. "You okay?"

Shaking my head no, I continued to stare. "I don't see them. Where did they go?"

"Who? You mean Chuck? He's by the pond."

David's oblivion fueled my anxiety. I felt my palms sweat as I opened and closed them methodically.

"He's not there," I shot back. "David, I need you to reassure me that he's safe." I stared at him, making direct eye contact.

He knew this look, and while sometimes he simply rolled his eyes at my concerns, it was clear I was seriously distraught. "I'll be right back."

I went back to the pile of dishes, finding myself unable to focus. I firmly held onto the side of the counter, watching as I saw David disappear along the edge of the woods. He finally came back through the side door.

"All good, Lar. They went for a walk behind the barn. The kid got bored with fishing."

He squeezed my shoulders and walked away. I sat down for a few minutes, feeling relieved and foolish.

I thought of the teachers, church goers, and neighbors who saw me on a regular basis as I grew up, wondering if any of them had ever suspected what was going on in our house, with my father and with all our family chaos.

For years, I would ask how it could have happened, trying to force myself to remember where my mother and sister were.

Chuck and that boy were a reenactment of my dad and me, but in my case, the outcome was not a simple walk in the woods when I got bored. It was an opportunity for my father to indulge himself in his young son.

———

Becoming more aware of my thoughts and emotions was a painful process. Without my long-standing ways of numbing, I was forced to feel, and if I were going to move forward, I believed I had to work through them.

No area of my life seemed protected from that new scrutiny. I had to rethink how I spent my days, and my money.

My shop had provided me with a sense of purpose and value, and I believed that without it, I had no way of defining who I was.

I thought back to the person I had been when I opened it, and it saddened me to think of the crippling anxiety and denial I lived with then.

"I think you should close the business. I don't think it serves you anymore," David said cautiously one day, obviously having thought it through.

David's words stung. I felt myself consumed with resentment.

He had struck a chord, and I felt guilty for my dwindling passion for what I had created. I was terrified to feel that much freedom, and to allow myself time to be still and discover new opportunities.

However, I listened and took action, deciding to close out what had been a ten-year tumultuous and addictive chapter.

On the fifteenth anniversary of our first lunch date, David and I were married at a favorite restaurant in New York City. Surrounded by twenty-five close friends and family, we joined hands as we honored who we once were and who we had become, both as individuals and as a couple. I thought of that day on the street when I first laid eyes on him, and the feelings that had stirred in me. As I stood facing him, I saw those same eyes, but with a new understanding and appreciation for all he had sacrificed and had been willing to tackle with me.

I finally believed I did not have to face the uncertainty of the future alone.

Chapter Nineteen

I felt the vibration of my phone in my back pocket. Needing a break from my uneasiness at a social event, I retreated to a quiet corner and found solace in the deep windowsill of the old stone farmhouse where guests drank champagne and toasted the holiday season. The text read, "How can we help Don Price?"

It came from a friend who knew my story, a philanthropist who regularly jumped in to assist with local causes. The name was not familiar, but a quick search told me what I needed to know: "Ulster Man Killed Father in Response to Sexual Abuse."

I sat motionless as I read the story. Don had been charged with murder after beating his father to death with a baseball bat. I read and reread those words, trying to take them in. He alleged his father sexually abused his brother, him, and his grandson—Don's own son. The story said he waited in the driveway of his parents' home until his father appeared, telling him he was there to kill him for what he had done. He proceeded to beat his father to death and then turned himself in.

The story's resemblance to what my own fantasies had been was uncanny. I felt incredible sadness for this man who had allowed his anger to consume him. Were we so different? This could have been me, if I had not chosen to follow a path of deeper healing rather than commit a crime.

I felt some of my own rage as I read his father's obituary, nauseated at the mention of his involvement with Toys for Tots, thinking of other pedophiles like Jerry Sandusky and the scores of priests and rabbis with unsupervised, even encouraged, access to children. I read that Don's brother had committed suicide, and my heart ached for how intolerable the situation must feel.

I wanted to meet Don face to face. I was uncertain as to why, or what good it would do, but decided to follow through on what my gut was telling me. David knew the story had had a deep effect on me, but I kept my plans hidden even from him. I called the jail where Don was being held and inquired about visiting hours.

"Next visiting day is Saturday. Get here early and register with the front desk."

I panicked briefly; Saturday was just two days away.

That Saturday, I left everything in the car except my keys, which I placed in one of the lockers lining a corridor off the jail lobby. As I registered with the officer on duty, he explained that since I was the first to arrive, I would have to allow, or not, any subsequent visitors who showed up to see Don. I became edgy as I asked what would happen if Don's family or friends showed up.

"Don't worry. We've had experiences where wives and girlfriends both arrive, and it creates a problem. It shouldn't be an issue for you."

I scanned the line for any signs of people there to see Don too, growing more anxious as the clock ticked closer to the appointed visiting hour. Just as I feared, the officer pointed me out to a woman who looked bewildered as she stared in my direction.

"Mr. Ruhl, can you please speak to Mr. Price's wife?"

She looked at me skeptically before asking, "Who are you and why are you here?"

My hands were shaky, and I suddenly felt I had overstepped my bounds.

"My name is Larry. I read about Don in the paper. Unfortunately, he and I have things in common, so I wanted to speak with him."

Her gaze shifted to something between compassion and sadness.

When they started making announcements, calling out the inmates' last names and instructing the specific visitors to enter the scanning machine, my self-doubt returned.

"How was Don when you last saw him?" I was hoping she'd give me a sign it was okay that I was there.

"I haven't seen him since he turned himself in. This is my first visit."

I don't belong here, I thought. "I think I should probably go and allow you to visit with him alone. I can come another time, or even write."

"No, please come in. I think Don would really like to meet you."

They shuttled us through the various holding areas before escorting us into the visiting room. Inmates were separated from visitors by a half-wall, allowing for brief displays of affection. I watched as the prisoners made their way down the corridor, recognizing Don immediately from his photo in the paper. From across the room, he looked at his wife, then at me with a puzzled look.

He leaned over and gave her a kiss, and once instructed by the guards, took his seat across the wall. After looking back and forth between his wife and me, he nodded in my direction, and asked her, "Who's that?"

I introduced myself, saying I read about his experience in the newspaper. His wife added that I was there because I too had been abused.

I kept my hands clenched in my lap, and my mouth was dry. I cleared my throat before attempting to speak.

"My father was like yours. I'm so sorry it happened to you too."

He remained fixated on my eyes. I held the intensity of the moment with him, feeling my chest tighten.

We understood our painful shared experiences, things that weren't natural or right. He slowly broke down, tears streaming down his face and into his thick beard. I thought of all the other survivors I had the opportunity to face in this way, connecting with our eyes through shared pain.

Afraid I'd start to cry too, I went on. "Don, you did what I chose not to do. I too thought of killing my father, but I chose a different path."

Wiping away tears, he spoke of his son and how special he was to him. He struggled to talk about his brother and his subsequent suicide. I listened and shared what I could.

A part of me wanted to stay with him, remain at his side and speak to the public defenders. I wanted to scream that no one, except survivors, could possibly understand how it all feels: the mountains of anger, confusion, and sadness.

I thanked Don for speaking with me and said my goodbyes. I felt a pang of guilt as my gratitude for being able to walk out a free man sank in. Before leaving the lobby, I deposited some money in Don's commissary account, a small, selfish gesture to remind myself of the potential consequences to our actions.

I got back in my car and sat for a while before feeling ready to drive. I thought of how survivors continue to struggle without reprieve, as they try to come to terms with their experiences.

I allowed myself to recall the anguish I felt when I held my own bat in my hands on that frigid night. Meeting Don had just shown me that outburst was the better way to work through the intolerable rage I carried.

I shifted my thoughts to the present day and to my friend Clio, with whom I had recently developed a strong bond, whose story I wished was impossible for us to have in common. Her experience and the way it unfolded was so intricately similar to mine that at times it left us dumbfounded. We'd stare at one another, offering a simple, "Me too," as we found comfort in knowing we weren't alone.

She understood what day-to-day life could feel like decades after the abuse occurred. The sound of a child screaming, the smell of someone's cologne or perfume, an expression of speech, or the close contact of a stranger or spouse—any of these things could trigger feelings of panic or confusing rage.

Clio and other survivors I've met allow me to navigate through life. They're a lifeline. They let me know I'm not alone with my feelings of doubt, fear, and terror.

Sharing our stories can mean the difference between life and death.

Acknowledgments

A quiet army of friends and confidants provided me with unwavering support. I offer my heartfelt gratitude to each of you. Melissa, Steve, Stephanie, and Luke Bauman. Daniel Michael, Ken Followell, Peter and Jen Buffett, Howard Fradkin, Eva Tenuto, Marianne Murray, Rich Rowley, Temple Jane Kennedy, Antonia Nelson, Kerry Smith, Chas Chilton, and Liam Robert. For their behind-the-scenes support and encouragement, I want to thank my sister, niece, and brother-in-law. I love you.

Benee Knauer, thank you for believing in my story, even when I was paralyzed by fear. Your guidance, compassion, and willingness to spend countless hours in that café on Sixteenth Street sustained me.

To Liese Mayer, thank you for stepping right in and taking me on as your brother without question. I love you.

Rob McQuilkin. You redefined the role of literary agent for me and showed me instantly that you are a man of your word. Thank you so much.

To my Central Recovery Press family. Thank you all for welcoming me with open arms. Valerie Killeen, Patrick Hughes, and Nancy Schenck. You met me with kindness, fearlessness, and determined dedication. I also want to offer a special thank you to Eliza Tutellier. You not only read with an open heart, but also believed in my story from day one. Your words have carried me through some very tough moments.

Kitty Sheehan. My heart is full as I contemplate the past year. Your talent as an editor and as a friend has been indispensible. I love you Sister Mary.

Jipala Kagan. You have helped me navigate the most turbulent waters. My life changed when I met you, and I continue to be awe-inspired by your commitment to this work. Thank you for being my most trusted guide.

To Linda Kawer. Every time I have tried to express my gratitude for what at times feels incomprehensible, I weep. My mind races through the past twelve years, and my heart aches with both pain and love, as I consider what was and what is now. This is my chance to say thank you.

To Marcelle Serouya. You not only gave me your incredible son, but you showed me what a mother could be. Nothing could disrupt the trust we found in one another. The influence you had on my life will remain with me forever, and I am truly grateful. I love you, Mom.

Nineteen years ago I took a risk and gave a stranger on the street my phone number. That man is now my husband. Jeffrey David Serouya, you make my spirit soar. It is no exaggeration to say that I would not still be alive had it not been for you. It's just us and nothing could be better. I love you to the moon and back.

Resources

www.1in6.org

www.takingbackourselves.org

www.RAINN.org

www.joyfulheartfoundation.org

www.yesican.org

www.tmiproject.org